Test Prep

Grade 2

Published by Spectrum®
An imprint of Carson-Dellosa Publishing LLC
Greensboro, North Carolina

Spectrum®
An imprint of Carson-Dellosa Publishing LLC
P.O. Box 35665
Greensboro, NC 27425 USA

ISBN 978-1-4838-1373-8

01-349147811

Table of Contents

What's Inside?

Spectrum Test Prep is designed to help you and your second grader prepare and plan for success on standardized tests.

Strategies

This workbook is structured around strategies. A strategy is a careful plan or method for achieving a particular goal, such as succeeding on a test. Strategies can be broad, general strategies about a test as a whole or a category of skills. Strategies can also be specific, providing step-by-step instructions on how to tackle a problem or offering guidelines on how to answer a question about a story. Learning how to apply a strategy gives test-takers a plan for how to approach a test as a whole and how to answer questions. This workbook offers a set of broader strategies as well as very specific strategies. General test-taking strategies apply to all tests, and should be used to help prepare for the test. Specific strategies for English Language Arts and Mathematics tests are divided into larger categories of skills students will encounter, such as reading literature or performing calculations. On each practice page, you will find even more specific strategies that apply to the skills.

Test Tips

Test Tips are included throughout the practice pages. While strategies offer a plan for answering test items, Test Tips offer ideas for how to apply each strategy or how to approach a type of question. There are general Test Tips that apply to all tests as well as specific Test Tips for English Language Arts and Mathematics tests.

Practice Pages

The workbook is divided into two sections, English Language Arts and Mathematics. Each section has practice activities that have questions similar to those that will appear on standardized tests. Also included are strategies and Test Tips to guide students. Students should use a pencil to complete these activities.

Strategy Review Pages

Strategy review pages give your student an opportunity to review and practice important strategies in each content area. These strategies cover the important skills students will encounter on tests in English Language Arts and Mathematics.

Answer Key

Answers for all of the practice pages and strategy review pages are found in an answer key at the end of the book.

Test-Taking Strategies

Being prepared is key to doing your best on test day. Read the tips below to help you prepare for tests.

In the days before the test...

- Keep up on your reading, worksheets, and assignments. Completing all your assigned work will help you be better prepared for the test.

- Don't wait until right before the test to review materials. Create a study schedule for the best result. That way, you can study a bit at a time and not all at once.

- Take advantage of sample items and practice tests. Complete these to practice for your test. If you run into concepts or skills that are new, ask a teacher or other adult.

The night before the test...

- Don't try to study everything all over again the night before. If you've been studying in the days before the test, all you need the night before is a light review of your notes. Remind yourself of the key ideas and practice a few skills, but don't study late into the night.

- Make sure you have all the materials you will need for the test, such as pencils, paper, and a calculator. Check with your teacher to make sure you know what tools to bring. Having everything ready the night before will make the morning less stressful.

- Get a good night's sleep the night before the test. If you are well rested, you will be more alert and able to do your best.

On the day of the test...

- Don't skip breakfast. If you are hungry, you won't be thinking about the test. You'll be thinking about lunch.

- Make sure you have at least two sharpened pencils with you and any other tools needed.

- Read all directions carefully. Make sure you understand how you are supposed to answer each question.

- For multiple choice questions, read all the possible answers before choosing one. If you know that some answers are wrong, cross them off. Even if you have to guess, this will eliminate some wrong answers.

- Once you choose or write an answer, double check it by reading the question again. Confirm that your answer is correct.

- Answer every part of a question. If a question asks you to show your work or to explain how you arrived at an answer, make sure you include that information.

- If you are stuck on a question, or unsure, mark it lightly with a pencil and move on. If you have time, you can come back. This is especially true on a timed test.

- Breathe! Remind yourself that you've prepared for the test and that you will do your best!

Strategies for English Language Arts Tests

Use details from a story or passage to show your understanding.
Authors choose details to include in their writing. Every detail is important. As you read, look for details. Think about why the author chose those details. Use them to understand what the author means.

Use details to make a picture in your mind as you read.
Authors use descriptive details to paint a picture for readers. As you read, try to picture in your mind what people, places, and events look like.

Look carefully at pictures.
Authors include pictures, photos, and text features like charts and webs to show something about the words on the page. As you read, use them to help you understand what you are reading.

Reread to answer questions.
If you don't know the answer to a question right away, don't worry! You can go back and read the story or passage again. As you reread, look for the answer to the question.

Ask questions as you read.
Careful readers stop once in a while to think about what they are reading. They ask questions like, *What was this paragraph about?* As you read, ask yourself questions to make sure you understand.

Pay attention to how parts of a story or passage connect and fit together.
Authors work hard to make sure the parts of their writing fit together. In a story, the characters, place, and events fit together. In nonfiction, authors usually keep connected ideas together.

When you write, use details to support main ideas.
If you write a story, include details that help the reader see, smell, and hear the characters, places, and events. If you write nonfiction, use details to support a main idea.

Plan your writing.
Make a plan before you start writing. For stories, make sure you choose characters, a setting, and events. Your story should have a beginning, middle, and end. For nonfiction, choose main ideas. Usually one to three main ideas is enough. Then, support each main idea with details that help explain.

Revise to make sure your writing makes sense. Then, edit to fix errors. Use what you know about nouns, verbs, adjectives, and adverbs to make correct choices when you edit.
After you finish your draft, you may have time to revise and edit. First, revise to make sure your words say what you want them to say. Then, check spelling, capitalization, punctuation, and grammar to catch and fix errors.

English Language Arts

Describe a Story
Reading: Literature

DIRECTIONS: Read the story. Then, answer the questions keeping the characters, setting, and what happens in mind.

Invisible Cassie

Cassie kicked at the dirty clothes on her floor. She was upset. Her dad told her to clean her room. Cassie wished she were invisible. Then, she wouldn't have to clean anything! If she were invisible, she would go to school and not do any work. She would stay up late. She would never have to take baths. Best of all, her brother couldn't pick on her. But, wait! If she were invisible, she wouldn't get any apple pie. No one would ask her to play. Cassie would never get to hug her grandparents. Maybe being invisible wouldn't be so much fun after all.

Strategy   Identify and make a list of the parts of a story: characters, setting, and what happens.

Test Tip   A story usually tells what characters think or how they feel.

1. **What is Cassie's problem in the beginning of the story?**

   (A) She wants to visit her grandparents.

   (B) She can't have any apple pie.

   (C) She has a brother who teases her.

   (D) She doesn't want to clean her room.

   What details in the story tell you about Cassie's problem? Choose all that apply.

   (A) "Cassie kicked at the dirty clothes on her floor."

   (B) "She was upset."

   (C) "Her dad told her to clean her room"

   (D) "Best of all, her brother couldn't pick on her."

2. **Write two details that tell why Cassie thinks being invisible is a good solution to her problem.**

   1. _____

   _____

   2. _____

   _____

3. **Who is the main character in the story?**

   (A) Cassie's dad

   (B) Cassie

   (C) Cassie's grandparents

   (D) Cassie's brother

   Write how you know.

   _____

   _____

   _____

   _____

4. **Which sentences from the story tell why Cassie wouldn't want to be invisible? Choose all that apply.**

   (A) "Best of all, her brother couldn't pick on her."

   (B) "If she were invisible she wouldn't get any apple pie."

   (C) "Cassie would never get to hug her grandparents."

   (D) "She would stay up late."

Name _____ Date _____

Describe a Story
Reading: Literature

DIRECTIONS: Read the story. Then, answer the questions using details from the story and the picture.

The Oldest

Sometimes, Sam likes being the oldest. He can stay up one hour later. He can go places by himself. He also gets a bigger allowance for helping around the house. When his friend Brennan asks him to spend the night, Sam's mom says yes. He even gets to stay at his friend's house to eat dinner sometimes. Sam thinks it's great that he can read, ride a bike, and spell better than his brother. Sam's sister loves when he reads stories to her. Sam likes it, too. When his mom needs help cooking, she asks Sam, because he is the oldest.

Sometimes, Sam doesn't like being the oldest. He has to babysit his sister. She likes to go where he does. He also has to act more like a grown-up. Sam always has more jobs to do around the house. He has to help wash the dishes and take out the trash. His brother and sister get help when they have to clean their rooms. Sam doesn't get help. Sam doesn't like to be the oldest when his brother and sister want him to play with them all the time.

Strategy Ask yourself Who, What, and Where questions to figure out the parts of a story.

Test Tip Look for who the story is mostly about to find the main character.

1. Who is the main character in the story?

Ⓐ Sam

Ⓑ Mom

Ⓒ Brennan

Ⓓ Sam's sister

Write how you know.

_____

_____

2. Which detail tells how Sam thinks or feels?

Ⓐ He likes to help his mother with the cooking.

Ⓑ He thinks his sister should read more stories.

Ⓒ He doesn't like it when he has to act like a grown-up.

Ⓓ He wants his parents to treat his brother like they treat him.

3. Write a detail from the story that tells how Sam's parents treat him like a grown-up.

4. What is this story mostly about?

_____

_____

5. The story is organized into two parts or ideas. The first part tells about why Sam likes being the oldest. The second part tells about why Sam _____ .

Ⓐ likes to have dinner at Brennan's house

Ⓑ helps his brother and sister clean their rooms

Ⓒ wants to play all the time

Ⓓ doesn't like being the oldest

English Language Arts

Recount Stories
Reading: Literature

DIRECTIONS: Read the story. Then, answer the questions using key details from the story.

Strategy | While reading, identify the lesson learned from the story. This is the moral of the story.

Adapted from "The Frog Who Wished to Be as Big as an Ox" by Aesop

One day, an ox was grazing in a meadow. Suddenly, he stepped on a young frog and crushed him to death. The frog's brothers and sisters ran to tell their mother what had happened.

"The monster that did it was such a size, Mother!" they said.

The mother was a vain old thing. She thought that she could easily make herself as large.

"Was it as big as this?" she asked, blowing and puffing herself out.

"Oh, much bigger than that," replied the young frogs.

"As this, then?" she cried, puffing and blowing again with all her might.

"No, mother," they said, "if you were to try till you burst yourself, you could never be so big."

That silly old frog! She tried to puff herself out still more, and burst herself indeed.

1. **These events from the story are out of order. Write the numbers 2, 3, 4, 5, 6, and 7 to retell the story in the correct order.**

   [1] An ox was grazing in a meadow.

   [ ] The frog's brothers and sisters ran home to tell their mother.

   [ ] The mother frog puffed and blew, and tried to make herself as big as an ox.

   [ ] The ox stepped on a frog and crushed it.

   [ ] The mother thought she could be as big as an ox.

   [ ] The frogs told their mother she could never be as big as the ox.

   [ ] The mother tried to puff herself out still more.

   [8] The mother frog burst.

2. **What do you think the moral of this story is?**

   Ⓐ Don't puff yourself up or you will burst.

   Ⓑ Don't step on frogs.

   Ⓒ Don't tell your mother when an ox crushes your brother.

   Ⓓ Don't try to be something you're not.

   Write why you think that is the lesson.

   _____

   _____

   _____

4. **Chose two adjectives that describe the mother frog.**

   Ⓐ silly

   Ⓑ brave

   Ⓒ proud

   Ⓓ smart

5. **What do you think the word vain means in the sentence, "The mother was a vain old thing."**

   _____

   _____

English Language Arts

Recount Stories
Reading: Literature

DIRECTIONS: Read the story. Then, answer the questions.

Strategy After reading the questions, reread the story and find the answers.

Adapted from "THE COFFEE-MAKING"
(an American Indian story)

One summer afternoon my mother left me alone in our wigwam while she went across the way to my aunt's home. A short while later, a hand lifted the canvas covering of the entrance. It was an old grandfather who had often told me legends of our people.

"Where is your mother, my little grandchild?" were his first words.

"My mother is soon coming back from my aunt's tepee," I replied.

"I shall wait for her return," he said, sitting on a mat.

At once I began to play the part of a kind hostess. I turned to my mother's coffeepot. Lifting the lid, I found nothing but coffee grounds in the bottom. I set the pot on a heap of cold ashes and filled it half full of warm Missouri River water. Then, I placed a small piece of bread in a bowl. I poured out a cup of worse than muddy warm water. I handed the light luncheon to the old warrior.

I was proud to have succeeded so well in serving refreshments to a guest all by myself. Before the old warrior had finished eating, my mother entered. She wondered where I had found coffee. She knew I had never made any before. She also knew that she had left the coffeepot empty. Answering the question in my mother's eyes, the warrior remarked, "My granddaughter made coffee on a heap of dead ashes, and served me the moment I came."

They both laughed, and mother said, "Wait a little longer, and I shall build a fire." They treated my best judgment, poor as it was, with the utmost respect.

6. **These events from the story are out of order. Write the numbers 2, 3, 4, 5, 6, and 7 to retell the story in the correct order.**

[1] The girl's mother left her alone in the wigwam.

[ ] The girl saw that there were only old coffee grounds in the coffee pot.

[ ] The girl placed a small piece of bread in a bowl.

[ ] The girl's mother came home and offered to make a fire.

[ ] An old grandfather came to the wigwam.

[ ] The girl poured warm river water into the coffee pot.

[ ] The girl served the coffee and bread to the grandfather.

[8] The girl's mother and the warrior treated her best judgment with respect.

7. **Choose two adjectives that describe the grandfather.**

(A) brave

(B) kind

(C) respectful

(D) mean

English Language Arts

Describe Characters' Responses
Reading: Literature

DIRECTIONS: Read the story. Then, answer the questions.

Strategy While reading, look for clue words after dialogue like *he said*, *replied*, and characters' names to know who is speaking. Try to see and hear the characters in your mind.

Summer Saturday

It was a beautiful Saturday morning. Austin asked, "Mom, can Daniel come over to play?"

"Sure," said Austin's mom. So Austin hopped on his bike and pedaled over to Daniel's house.

The door opened and Daniel's mom looked at Austin. "Good morning, Austin," she said. "I bet you are here to see Daniel." She let Austin in and he quickly found Daniel watching TV.

"Hey," said Austin. "Do you want to come over?"

"I'm watching this," said Daniel without looking away from the screen. Austin glanced at the screen. It was a cartoon he had seen a million times.

"Come on, Daniel!" he said. "We can ride bikes." Daniel did not answer. Austin sat down and watched the cartoon for a minute. Then, he got up again.

"How about we go to the park," Austin suggested.

"No," said Daniel. "I just want to relax today."

Austin thought again. "Swimming?"

"No. Relaxing," Daniel replied.

"Come on, Daniel," Austin tried again. "Let's do something."

Daniel was not budging. "OK," Austin said. "I'm going to go see if someone else can play."

1. How did Austin want to spend the day?

(A) watching TV

(B) playing outside

(C) playing on the computer

(D) at the movies

2. Why didn't Daniel want to do anything Austin suggested?

_____

_____

3. Which detail tells you how Daniel feels about going outside?

(A) "So Austin hopped on his bike and pedaled over to Daniel's house."

(B) " 'Hey,' said Austin. 'Do you want to come over?' "

(C) " 'No,' said Daniel. 'I just want to relax today.' "

(D) "Daniel looked away from the TV for a second."

4. What suggestions did Austin make to try and change Daniel's mind? Choose two.

(A) swimming

(B) riding bikes

(C) going bowling

(D) going to the carnival

5. How did Austin solve his problem?

_____

English Language Arts

Characters' Responses
Reading: Literature

DIRECTIONS: Read the story. Then, answer the questions.

> ## Strategy
> As you read, find details that tell what the characters do. Then look for details that give reasons for characters' actions.

The Ant and the Grasshopper

Once upon a time there was an ant and a grasshopper.

Every day, the ant would work hard. He would collect bits of food and pile them up in his ant hole. Back and forth he went. He collected berries and nuts.

Every day, the grasshopper watched the ant hard at work. He laughed as the ant carried bits of food that were twice his size.

In the autumn, the leaves fell and the air grew cool. The ant continued to gather food and put it in his hole. The grasshopper found new things to explore.

Soon, the winter came. The ant crawled down his hole. He nibbled on a berry here and a nut there. It was a cozy home. The grasshopper, too, crawled into his hole. There was a lot of dirt in his hole, but nothing to eat.

Grasshopper hopped through the frozen grass to Ant's hole, and wriggled in.

"Hello, Ant!" Grasshopper said with a big smile.

"Why, hello, Grasshopper," replied Ant. "How are you?"

"Oh, not so good," said Grasshopper. "My hole is not cozy. And I have no food for the winter."

"Yes," said Ant. "That is a shame. But while I was working all year to fill my hole with food for the winter, what did you do? You played and you explored. And you laughed at me."

Grasshopper was embarrassed. "Yes," he said, "but you are such a kind Ant. Couldn't you share some of your food with me?"

Ant thought for a moment. He shook his head. "If I share my food with you, what will you learn?" he said. "I am sorry, Grasshopper, but I will not share my food with you."

Grasshopper was sad. He left Ant's hole slowly. He hoped Ant would change his mind. For the rest of the winter, Grasshopper was very hungry. He found a blade of frozen grass here and there, but it was not very much.

Soon enough, spring arrived. Ant crawled out of his hole and soon began his work again. When he looked around, he saw Grasshopper jumping through the grass. But, this time Grasshopper had a large berry on his back. He had learned his lesson and was gathering food to put in his hole. Ant was very proud of him.

English Language Arts

Characters' Responses
Reading: Literature

1. Why did Ant gather food all year?

(A) so he would have food in the winter

(B) because he was always hungry

(C) to share it with the other insects

(D) so no other insects would have food

2. At the beginning of the story, what was Grasshopper's opinion about gathering food?

_____

_____

3. What happened to Grasshopper when winter came?

_____

_____

4. How did Ant feel when Grasshopper came to him for food?

(A) he was happy to help

(B) he didn't want to help, because he wanted Grasshopper to learn a lesson

(C) he didn't want to help, because he didn't want to share his food

(D) he didn't want to help, because Grasshopper was mean

5. What lessons do you think this story teaches?

_____

_____

_____

_____

English Language Arts

Understand Poetry
Reading: Literature

DIRECTIONS: Read the poem. Then, answer the questions using key details from the poem.

Strategy | Read each stanza, or part, of the poem carefully. Ask and answer the question *What is this stanza about?* before moving on to the next stanza.

Test Tip | Read the poem quietly to yourself. Listen for the rhythm and rhyme of the words as you read.

From "The Arrow and the Song" *by Henry W. Longfellow*

I shot an arrow into the air,
It fell to earth, I do not know where;
It flew so fast that my sight
Could not follow it in its flight.

I sang a song into the air,
It fell to earth, I do not know where;
Because who has sight so sharp and strong
That it can follow the flight of song?

Long, long after, in an oak
I found the arrow, it had not broke;
And the song, from beginning to end,
I found again in the heart of a friend.

---

1. A rhyme pattern tells which words at the end of a line rhyme. What lines rhyme in stanza 1?

(A) 1 and 3

(B) 1 and 2; 3 and 4

(C) 1 and 4

(D) none

2. Write the pairs of rhyming words the poet uses.

Stanza 1: _____ _____

_____ _____

Stanza 2: _____ _____

_____ _____

Stanza 3: _____ _____

_____ _____

3. How are poems organized differently from stories?

_____

_____

4. Reread the first stanza. Write a sentence that describes what happens in that stanza.

_____

_____

5. What did the poet send into the air in the second stanza?

(A) a song

(B) an arrow

(C) a friend

(D) an oak

Write how you know.

_____

_____

_____

Name _____ Date _____

English Language Arts

Understand Poetry
Reading: Literature

DIRECTIONS: Read each poem. Then, answer the questions using key details from the poem.

Strategy   As you read, mark the lines that rhyme.

Sweets, sweets are fun to eat
But too much yummy
can rot your teeth
and hurt your tummy

6. What rhyming words are in this poem?

_____

_____

7. What message is the poet trying to tell you?

Ⓐ Sweets are fun to eat.

Ⓑ You should eat sweets every day.

Ⓒ Sweets taste good, but aren't good for you.

Ⓓ Brush your teeth each day or you will
get cavities.

Allison the alligator
Absolutely adored acrobats.
Allison always attended any acrobatic affair
And as the acrobats ascended above
Allison always asked,
"How do I get up there?"

8. What is repeated in this poem?

Ⓐ the word alligator

Ⓑ the short a sound

Ⓒ rhyming words

Ⓓ the *ing* sound

Hey diddle, diddle
The cat and the fiddle,
The cow jumped over the moon.
The little dog laughed
To see such sport,
And the dish ran away with the spoon.

9. How is the last line of the poem different from the others?

_____

_____

10. List the rhyming words from the poem.

_____   _____

_____   _____

11. How do the nonsense words "diddle diddle" affect this poem? Choose two.

Ⓐ You know from the first line that it's
a silly poem.

Ⓑ The words make the poem more realistic.

Ⓒ Silly words make a poem fun to read.

Ⓓ Nonsense words always rhyme.

English Language Arts

Describe Parts of a Story
Reading: Literature

DIRECTIONS: Read the story. Then, answer the questions using key details from the story.

Lazy Time

Sally and Ned are swaying slowly in the family swing. The air is crisp. Sally puts her arm around Ned and snuggles into his shaggy body. Ned's tongue licks Sally's hand that lies on her blue-jeaned leg. They watch a slow ladybug crawl underneath a pile of old, brown leaves. One red leaf drifts to the top of the ladybug's leaf pile. Ned's graying ears stand up as a *V* of geese honks goodbye. The sky slowly turns from blue, to pink, to purple, to black.

The first star shines as Sally's mom calls her in to eat. Sally gives a last push as she slides out of the swing. She walks to the back door of the house. Ned leaps down. He barks once at a rabbit and chases after Sally. She smiles and rubs Ned's head as they walk into the warm house together.

Strategy

Most stories have the same parts: characters, settings, and events. As you read, identify these parts and make a list of each one.

Test Tip

Details, especially ones that use the five senses, help you picture a story more clearly in your mind. Look for these details to understand the story.

1. The setting is _____.

- (A) the main problem in a story
- (B) where and when a story takes place
- (C) the reason the author wrote a story
- (D) the picture with a story

2. This story most likely takes place in _____.

- (A) a made-up time
- (B) the past
- (C) the present
- (D) the future

Write how you know.

_____

_____

3. Write two key details that tell you that the story takes place in the autumn.

_____

_____

_____

4. What do the details tell you about Ned?

_____

_____

5. What does the beginning of the story introduce?

- (A) It introduces the characters.
- (B) It describes the setting.
- (C) It describes the plot of the story.
- (D) It tells how the story ends.

Name _____ Date _____

English Language Arts

Describe Parts of a Story
Reading: Literature

DIRECTIONS: Read the story. Then, answer the questions using key details from the story.

Strategy   As you read, identify the problem the characters face. Write the problem down. Then, find details that tell how the characters solve the problem.

Skating

It was a sunny, spring day. Jason could not wait for Tasha to show him how to use his new inline skates. Jason had always wanted skates. He finally got them for his birthday. Now, he was ready for his first lesson. Jason and Tasha went to the park.

When they got to the park, they saw Michael. Michael raced by the slower skaters and made a face at them. "Show-off," Jason said.

Suddenly, Jason heard a loud crash on the other side of the park.

"What was that?" asked Tasha.

Michael limped around the corner. He was covered with twigs and leaves.

"I don't think we have to worry about show-offs anymore," Jason said with a smile.

1. **Describe the setting of the story.**

_____

_____

2. **Who are the two main characters in the story?**

   (A) Michael and Tasha

   (B) Jason and Michael

   (C) Jason and Tasha

   (D) the skates

Write how you know.

_____

_____

_____

Test Tip

A story has a beginning, a middle, and an end. The problem is usually told in the beginning and solved by the end.

3. **How does the beginning introduce the story?**

_____

_____

_____

4. **Which key detail tells you the problem in the story?**

   (A) "Jason had always wanted skates."

   (B) "Jason and Tasha went to the park."

   (C) "Michael raced by the slower skaters and made a face at them."

   (D) "Michael limped around the corner."

5. **Why did Jason smile at the end of the story? How was his problem solved?**

   (A) Jason was a good skater.

   (B) Tasha went home.

   (C) Michael raced past them.

   (D) Michael would not be showing off anymore.

Compare and Contrast
Reading: Literature

DIRECTIONS: Read the stories. Then, answer the questions.

Strategy Read to identify details that are similar and details that are different between two stories. Ask yourself, *How are the characters, settings, and events of the stories alike? How are they different?*

Adapted from *Snow White*

Snow White's stepmother was a wicked woman. But, she was also very beautiful. The magic mirror told her this every day, whenever she asked it. "Mirror, mirror on the wall, who is the loveliest of all?" The reply was always; "You are, your Majesty." The awful day came when she heard it say, "Snow White is the loveliest of all."

The stepmother was angry and wild with jealousy. She began plotting to get rid of Snow White. She bribed one of her trusty servants with a rich reward to take Snow White into the forest far away from the castle. Then, he was to put her to death. The greedy servant was attracted to the reward. He agreed to do this deed and led the innocent little girl away. However, the man's courage failed him. Leaving Snow White sitting beside a tree, he mumbled an excuse and ran off.

Snow White was alone in the dark forest. She began to cry bitterly. She heard strange sounds and rustlings that made her heart thump. At last, overcome by tiredness, she fell asleep curled under a tree.

Adapted from *The Story of Princess Hase-Hime* (a Japanese fairy tale)

There was only one person who was not pleased by Princess Hase-Hime, and that was her stepmother. She had the embarrassment of seeing her stepdaughter rise to power and honor. The young girl was favored and admired by the whole Court. The stepmother's envy and jealousy burned in her heart like fire. She created many lies to tell her husband about Hase-Hime. He would not believe her tales and sharply told her she was wrong.

At last her husband went on a trip to a far-off land. The stepmother ordered one of her old servants to take the innocent Hase-Hime to the Hibari Mountains. This was the wildest part of the country. She told the old man to kill the girl there. The servant could not disobey. But, he knew the young girl was innocent of all the things her stepmother had invented. He was determined to save the girl. Unless he killed her however, he could not return to his cruel ruler. So, he made up his mind to stay in the wilderness with the young princess and keep her safe.

beautiful	woods	mountains	wicked stepmother
anger and jealousy	plot to kill girl	magic mirror	bribed servant
servant did not kill girl	left girl alone	stayed with girl	ordered servant
favored and admired			

Snow White   **Both**   **Hase-Hime**

Compare and Contrast
Reading: Literature

Strategy — Draw a chart or diagram to organize the characters, setting, and events in each story. A Venn diagram can help you see details that are the same and details that are different.

Test Tip — Read each question carefully to decide if it is asking you about one story or both stories.

2. **Why did Snow White's stepmother want her killed?**

   Ⓐ Everyone favored and admired Snow White.

   Ⓑ Snow White was not a real princess.

   Ⓒ Snow White was more beautiful.

   Ⓓ She wanted Snow White's money.

   Write how you know.

   _____

   _____

   _____

   _____

   _____

3. **Why did Hase-Hime's stepmother want her killed?**

   _____

   _____

   Write how you know.

   _____

   _____

   _____

   _____

4. **Which key details helped you answer question 3? Choose two.**

   Ⓐ "She had the embarrassment of seeing her stepdaughter rise to power and honor."

   Ⓑ "The stepmother's envy and jealousy burned in her heart like fire."

   Ⓒ "At last her husband went on a trip to a far-off land."

   Ⓓ "The servant could not disobey."

Test Tip — When comparing two stories, be sure to look for what is the same and for what is different.

5. **Use what you wrote in the Venn diagram to write a sentence that shows how the two stories are alike.**

   _____

   _____

   _____

6. **Use what you wrote in the Venn diagram to write a sentence that shows how the two stories are different.**

   _____

   _____

   _____

   _____

Use Key Details
Reading: Informational Text

DIRECTIONS: Read the passage. Then, answer the questions using key details from the passage.

Dolphins and Sharks

Dolphins and sharks both live in the ocean, but they are very different. There are about 40 different kinds of dolphins. Dolphins are mammals. Mammals are warm-blooded. This means that their bodies stay the same temperature even when the water is very cold. Mammals also give birth to live babies. A dolphin baby is called a calf. A mother dolphin can have only one calf at a time. A calf will stay with its mother for up to eight years. Dolphins have lungs for breathing. They breathe through a blowhole on their heads. This means that they must come to the surface often to get air. Dolphins communicate by making whistles, clicks, and squeaks.

Sharks are not mammals. They are fish. This means that they are cold-blooded. Sharks breathe through gills. They do not need to go to the surface for air. There are over 400 different kinds of sharks. Some sharks lay eggs like birds. In some sharks, eggs hatch and babies, called pups, grow inside the mother. And some sharks grow pups inside their bodies like dolphins. Sharks can have up to 100 pups at a time! Shark pups do not stay with their mother after they are born. Sharks and dolphins live in the same oceans, but they are very different.

Strategy — To identify the main idea, read the first and last sentence in the passage. The main idea is often introduced in the first sentence and repeated in the last sentence.

Test Tip — Passages give information and facts about a topic. A main idea is what a passage is mostly about. Look for facts that are about one topic—that is likely the main idea.

1. **What is the main idea of this passage?**

   Ⓐ Dolphins are mammals, but sharks are fish.

   Ⓑ Dolphins have lungs, but sharks have gills.

   Ⓒ Dolphins and sharks are very different.

   Ⓓ Dolphins and sharks both live in the ocean.

   Write how you know.

   _____

   _____

   _____

   _____

   _____

2. **What makes mammals different from fish? Choose two answers.**

   Ⓐ Mammals are warm blooded, but fish are cold blooded.

   Ⓑ Mammals give live birth, but fish lay eggs.

   Ⓒ Mammals are dolphins, but fish are sharks.

   Ⓓ Mammals communicate, but fish don't.

3. **Write a question that uses the key detail, "There are over 400 different kinds of sharks."**

   _____

   _____

4. **How are some sharks like birds?**

   _____

Use Key Details
Reading: Informational Text

DIRECTIONS: Read the passage. Then, answer the questions using key details from the passage.

India

In the United States, most people speak English. In India, there are more than 1,000 different languages. This has caused many problems. Many of the people speak the words in different ways. Hindi was chosen as the main language to solve the problem. However, it is still hard for people to talk to each other.

There are many ways to let others know what you think without using words. Some actions mean different things in India. For example, to show an older person that you respect him, bow down and touch his feet. If you want to be rude, sit with the bottoms of your shoes showing. To show you are clean, never wear your shoes in the house. If you don't want to be polite, point at your feet.

Strategy   Write the main idea down and then list 2 or 3 key details that support it.

Test Tip   A key detail tells more information about the main idea. Key details support the main idea of the story.

5. **What is the main idea of the passage?**

(A) It is fun to live in India.

(B) Learning to read is important.

(C) Never point at your feet or show the bottom of your shoes.

(D) In India, there are many ways to let others know what you think without words.

Which sentence helps you identify the main idea?

_____

_____

_____

6. **Based on the passage, what is rude in India?**

(A) never wearing your shoes in the house

(B) learning how to read

(C) sitting with the bottoms of your shoes showing

(D) going to the store

Write how you know.

_____

_____

_____

7. Write a question that uses the key detail, ". . . bow down and touch an older person's feet."

_____

Write how you know.

_____

_____

_____

8. **In India, how would a person show he or she is clean?**

(A) They point to their feet.

(B) They bow down and touch your feet.

(C) They do not wear shoes in the house.

(D) They show the bottoms of their shoes.

Find Word Meanings
Reading: Informational Text

DIRECTIONS: Read the passage. Then, answer the questions.

> Horses are beautiful animals. Most horses have smooth, shiny coats. They have long manes and tails. Their hair may be brown, black, white, yellow, or spotted. Sometimes, horses neigh, or make a loud, long cry. Horses need to be groomed, or brushed, every day. This helps keep them clean. Many people keep horses as pets or to work on farms. Some people enjoy riding them for fun. Horses are wonderful animals.

Strategy Circle words in the passage that you do not know. Then, read the passage and draw boxes around words in the passage that help you find the meaning of the unknown words.

Test Tip When you come across a new word, use the words around it to help you find its meaning.

1. **What does the word neigh mean?**
   - (A) make a loud, long cry
   - (B) no
   - (C) whistle loudly
   - (D) talk in horse language

2. **What might a spotted horse look like?**

   _____

   _____

   _____

3. **What is another word for groomed?**
   - (A) loud
   - (B) worked
   - (C) brushed
   - (D) spotted

Test Tip

When comparing two stories, be sure to look for what is the same and for what is different.

DIRECTIONS: Read the sentences. Then, choose the word that fits in both sentences.

4. _____ to the left.

   The _____ on this pencil broke.
   - (A) point
   - (B) eraser
   - (C) shine
   - (D) top

5. The boat began to _____.

   Dad washed the dishes in the _____.
   - (A) wait
   - (B) tub
   - (C) sink
   - (D) pan

6. Hit the _____ with the hammer.

   The _____ on my little finger is broken.
   - (A) tack
   - (B) nail
   - (C) skin
   - (D) wood

English Language Arts

Find Word Meanings
Reading: Informational Text

DIRECTIONS: Read the sentences. Then, choose the word that means the same as the underlined word.

Strategy | Use the general meaning of the sentence to find the meaning of unknown words. The unknown word should connect, or relate, to what is happening in the sentence.

Test Tip | Try each word in place of the underlined word in the sentence.

7. Jane's mom wrote a <u>memo</u> about her daughter's illness to the teacher.
   - (A) message
   - (B) drink
   - (C) pencil
   - (D) ticket

8. Susan was <u>grateful</u> that her dad drove her to school because it was raining.
   - (A) thankful
   - (B) sad
   - (C) angry
   - (D) finished

Write how you know.

_____

_____

_____

_____

9. The brothers <u>bellowed</u> for their dog to come home.
   - (A) cared
   - (B) yelled
   - (C) heard
   - (D) whispered

10. Grandma asked me to <u>divide</u> the cookies evenly between the children.
   - (A) use
   - (B) bake
   - (C) split
   - (D) stand

Write how you know.

_____

_____

_____

_____

11. I always keep my room <u>immaculate</u>. Everything is in its place.
   - (A) bad
   - (B) pretty
   - (C) clean
   - (D) dark

12. The Grand Canyon is an <u>immense</u> hole in the ground.
   - (A) huge
   - (B) tiny
   - (C) ready
   - (D) round

Describe Connections
Reading: Informational Text

DIRECTIONS: Read the passage. Then, answer the questions using key details from the passage.

How to Make a Peanut Butter and Jelly Sandwich
You will need peanut butter, jelly, and two pieces of bread. First, spread peanut butter on one piece of bread. Next, spread jelly on the other piece. Then, put the two pieces of bread together. Next, cut the sandwich in half. Finally, eat your sandwich and enjoy!

Strategy   Number each step of the process in order (1, 2, 3) to make sure you understand the sequence, or order, of the process.

Test Tip   Words like *first*, *next*, and *finally* are clues to the order of the steps.

1. What is this paragraph explaining?

Ⓐ how to make peanut butter

Ⓑ how to cut a sandwich

Ⓒ how to make a peanut butter and jelly sandwich

Ⓓ how to put bread together

Write how you know.

_____

_____

2. What does the paragraph say to do after you spread peanut butter on one piece of bread?

_____

3. Why is the first sentence important?

_____

_____

Can you take out the first sentence? Why or why not?

_____

_____

4. What is the last step in the paragraph?

Ⓐ Put the two pieces of bread together.

Ⓑ Cut the sandwich.

Ⓒ Eat and enjoy your sandwich.

Ⓓ Spread peanut butter on one piece of bread.

5. What would happen if you put the two pieces of bread together before spreading the jelly?

Write how you know.

_____

_____

_____

6. Which step could you leave out if you wanted to?

Ⓐ Spread the peanut butter.

Ⓑ Spread the jelly.

Ⓒ Put the two pieces of bread together.

Ⓓ Cut the sandwich in half.

Describe Connections
Reading: Informational Text

DIRECTIONS: Read the passage.

Insects in Winter

In the summertime, insects can be seen buzzing and fluttering around us. But as winter's cold weather begins, the insects seem to disappear. Do you know where they go? Many insects find a warm place to spend the winter.

Ants try to dig deep into the ground. Some beetles stack up in piles under rocks or dead leaves.

Female grasshoppers do not even stay around for winter. In the fall, they lay their eggs and die. The eggs hatch in the spring.

Bees also try to protect themselves from the winter cold. Honeybees gather in a ball in the middle of their hive. The bees stay in this tight ball trying to stay warm.

Winter is very hard for insects, but each spring the survivors come out, and the buzzing and fluttering begin again.

Strategy

To make connections, identify the topic of the passage. Then, list the main idea and 2 or 3 key details that support it. Use the list to understand how the ideas in the passage are connected.

Test Tip

When you read passages that give information, notice how the information connects. This passage connects different insects by telling what they do in winter.

1. Use the passage to fill in the topic sentence below. Fill in the rest of the ovals with supporting details.

Many insects find a _____ place to spend the _____.

2. **How are the details about insects connected in this passage?**
   (A) They are about ants.
   (B) They are about beetles.
   (C) They are about how insects survive winter.
   (D) They are about how insects gather food.

3. **Write how the details support the main idea.**

   _____

   _____

4. **Which insect does not find a warm place in winter?**
   (A) ants
   (B) beetles
   (C) bees
   (D) grasshoppers

English Language Arts

Identify Author's Purpose
Reading: Informational Text

DIRECTIONS: Read the passage. Then, answer the questions using key details from the passage.

Therapy Dogs

Dogs can help people get better after they've been sick. These special dogs are called therapy dogs.

The dogs' owners bring them into hospital rooms. They let people meet the dogs. Sometimes, the dogs go right up to the beds. People can pet the dogs, brush them, and talk to them. Studies have shown that being with dogs and other animals can help people heal faster.

Not every dog is a good choice for this important job. A therapy dog must be calm and friendly. Some therapy dog owners feel that their pets were born to help sick people get well again.

Strategy   While you read a detail in the passage, ask yourself *Why did the author include this detail? What is the author trying to tell me as a reader?*

Test Tip   The author's purpose is the reason he or she wrote a passage. Authors often write passages to give information.

1. **Which sentence best summarizes the author's main point?**

   (A) Therapy dogs like to be brushed.

   (B) Therapy dogs are calm and friendly.

   (C) Therapy dogs help sick people get better.

   (D) Therapy dogs enjoy visiting people in hospitals.

   Write how you know. Which sentence in the passage supports this as the main idea?

   _____

   _____

2. **Choose two details to support the author's claim that not every dog is a good choice to be a therapy dog.**

   (A) "Sometimes, the dogs go right up to the beds."

   (B) "A therapy dog must be calm and friendly."

   (C) "People can pet the dogs, brush them, and talk to them."

   (D) "Some therapy dog owners feel that their pets were born to help sick people get well again."

3. **Write the reason the author wrote this passage.**

   _____

   _____

4. **Would an excited and unfriendly dog make a good therapy dog? Write how you know.**

   _____

   _____

5. **Write the sentence that tells how therapy dogs help sick people.**

   _____

   _____

6. **Where could you look to find more information about therapy dogs?**

   (A) a website about types of dogs

   (B) a website about helper animals

   (C) the dictionary

   (D) a map

English Language Arts

Identify Author's Purpose
Reading: Informational Text

DIRECTIONS: Read the passage. Then, answer the questions.

> **Jellyfish**
> Jellyfish come in all sizes and colors. Some are only one inch across. Other jellyfish are five feet wide. Some are orange. Others are red. Some jellyfish have no color at all. Gently poke one type of jellyfish with a stick, and it will glow. However, do not let any jellyfish touch you, because they can sting!

Strategy — While reading, identify the main idea of a passage. Use the main idea to find the author's purpose, or what information the author wants to share with readers.

Test Tip — Key details support the author's main idea.

7. **Which sentence best summarizes the author's main point?**

   (A) Jellyfish can sting.

   (B) There are many kinds of jellyfish.

   (C) Some jellyfish are orange.

   (D) Jellyfish can hide.

   Write the sentence that tells you the main point.

   _____

   _____

8. **Write two key details that support the author's main point.**

   _____

   _____

9. **Why did the author write this passage?**

   (A) To give an opinion about jellyfish.

   (B) To explain how jellyfish sting.

   (C) To describe different kinds of jellyfish.

   (D) To tell a story with jellyfish as characters.

Write how you know.

_____

_____

10. **Write the key detail that supports the author's claim that you should never touch a jellyfish.**

   _____

   _____

11. **Choose two facts the author used to support the idea that jellyfish come in all sizes.**

   (A) Some are only one inch across.

   (B) Other jellyfish are five feet wide.

   (C) Some are orange.

   (D) Others are red.

12. **How would the passage change if the author did not use facts to support the main point?**

   _____

   _____

   _____

Use Text Features
Reading: Informational Text

DIRECTIONS: Write or choose the correct answer.

Strategy | Use text features such as the table of contents, glossary, illustrations, and headings to find information. Read the text feature carefully to know what kind of information is given.

Test Tip | When you are putting words in alphabetical order, look at the next letter in the word if the first letters are the same.

1. **Which set of words is in the order they would appear in a glossary?**

   Ⓐ cat, dog, light, star

   Ⓑ dog, cat, light, star

   Ⓒ star, light, cat, dog

   Ⓓ light, cat, star, dog

   Write how you know.

   _____

   _____

2. **The guide words at the top of your glossary page are "face–fish." Which word will you find on the page?**

   Ⓐ full

   Ⓑ time

   Ⓒ enough

   Ⓓ factory

   Write how you know.

   _____

   _____

   _____

3. **Which heading would you look under to find out what sharks eat?**

   Ⓐ Sharks Are Everywhere

   Ⓑ A Shark's Body

   Ⓒ Dinner Time!

   Ⓓ Predator Or Prey?

DIRECTIONS: Use the Table of Contents and Index to answer questions 4 and 5.

TABLE OF CONTENTS	INDEX
Painting 3	colors 8, 22, 31
Drawing 14	museums . 2, 10, 19, 35
Index 53	pencil 16
Glossary 57	watercolor paints . . . 5

4. **On what page does the chapter on drawing start?**

   Ⓐ page 3

   Ⓑ page 14

   Ⓒ page 53

   Ⓓ page 57

5. **If you wanted to learn the meaning of the word docent, which page would you turn to?**

   _____

   Write how you know.

   _____

   _____

   _____

Name _____   Date _____

Use Text Features
Reading: Informational Text

DIRECTIONS: Read the passage. Then, answer the questions.

Strategy Look at illustrations and other images carefully and compare the information in the illustration to the information in the passage. Is there new information in the image? Or does it match information in the passage?

Signing

People who may not be able to hear or speak well use sign language. They use their hands instead of their voices to talk. Their hands make signals to show different letters, words, and ideas. For example, to say the word *love*, cross your arms over your chest.

Other people use sign language, too. Have you ever watched a football game? The referees use hand signals to let you know what has happened in the game, such as a foul or time-out. Have you ever watched a police officer direct traffic? The police officer can use sign language to tell cars to stop and go.

Guess who else uses sign language? You! You wave your hand when you say hello and good-bye. You nod your head up and down to say *yes*. You shake your head back and forth to say *no*. You use your fingers to point and show which way to go. We use our hands and body to make signals all of the time!

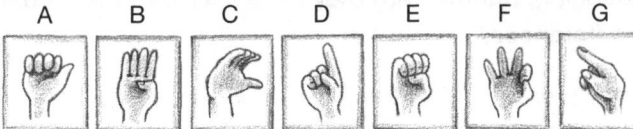

A   B   C   D   E   F   G

6. What is the main idea of the passage?

(A) People who have trouble hearing use sign language.

(B) People can write using sign language.

(C) There are many children's games that use sign language.

(D) It is hard to use sign language.

7. Which key detail does the picture help support?

(A) "People use their hands to make signals for different words, letters, and ideas."

(B) "The police officer can use sign language to tell cars to stop and go."

(C) "We use our hands and body to make signals all of the time!"

(D) "You shake your head back and forth to say no."

8. Write a caption that could go beneath the picture.

_____

_____

TABLE OF CONTENTS		INDEX	
Alabama	2	education	7, 15, 19, 27
Alaska	12	industry	5, 23
Arizona	25	population	4, 17, 26, 32
Index	36	resources	6, 13, 25

9. If you were doing a report on education in Alaska, which pages would you use?

_____

_____

Write how you know.

_____

_____

English Language Arts

Compare Two Passages
Reading: Informational Text

DIRECTIONS: Read the passages. Then, answer the questions.

> **Strategy**
>
> When you read two passages on the same topic, identify details that are the same and details that are different. Underline details that are the same in both passages. Circle details that are different.

Teachers Learn
To be a teacher, you have to be very smart. You have to learn and be able to teach about almost anything. Teachers work very hard. They plan lessons, grade papers, write report cards, and help students do their work. Some teachers teach only one subject. Other teachers teach many different subjects. Teaching is a very hard job.

Teachers Care
To be a teacher, you have to be very caring. You have to support children and be able to help them learn almost anything. Teachers work very hard. They plan for students to be successful. They get to read all of the interesting things children write. They help children become better learners. Some teachers teach only a few children. Other teachers teach many children. Teaching is a very rewarding job.

1. **Both passages are about teaching, but how are they different? Use the T-chart to list key ideas from both passages that show these differences.**

The author of passage 1 thinks that teachers . . .	The author of passage 2 thinks that teachers . . .

2. **How are these two passages alike?**
   - (A) They both tell how teaching is a hard job.
   - (B) They both tell how teaching is a rewarding job.
   - (C) They both tell how teachers work hard.
   - (D) They both tell how teachers plan lessons.

3. **Both passages tell about teachers, but each has a different focus. What is the focus of the first passage?**

   _____

   _____

   What is the focus of the second passage?

   _____

   _____

English Language Arts

Compare Two Passages
Reading: Informational Text

DIRECTIONS: Read the passages. Then, answer the questions.

Strategy When comparing two passages, identify and write down the topic of each passage. Then, write the main idea of each topic. Are the main ideas the same? Are they different?

Growing Dinner

Do you know where the food on your dinner table came from? It most likely came from a grocery store. But, what if you could grow your own dinner?

Planting and caring for a garden is an easy and fun thing to do. You first have to find a good spot for your garden. The spot should be sunny and protected from animals. You can use almost any container for gardening. Whether you put your garden in a container or dig it into the ground, you will need good soil.

Once you have your spot and your soil, you can plant your vegetables. You can start your vegetables from seeds or from small plants. Water your plants and pull the weeds. In a few weeks, you'll have some delicious vegetables. You can cook them up for dinner or eat them raw for a snack!

Gardening Fun

Gardening is a fun hobby. Many people enjoy the feeling of digging in the earth. Others enjoy the peace and quiet of being outside in nature. Whatever the reason, anybody can become a gardener.

Some people like to plant vegetables. Others like to plant flowers. The people who work at nurseries, or plant stores, will know which plants grow best where you live.

Once you know what you want to plant, you are on your way to becoming a gardener! Find a good, sunny spot. Put down some nice, rich soil. Bury your seeds, or put in your small plants. Then, all you have to do is water and pull out any weeds that grow. The insects and birds will love your garden as much as you do!

4. **Write three important facts from the first passage, "Growing Dinner."**

_____

_____

_____

_____

_____

5. **Write two key details from "Gardening Fun" that support the main idea "Gardening is a fun hobby."**

_____

_____

_____

6. **What are both passages mainly about?**

(A) the kinds of containers used for gardens

(B) different types of gardens

(C) the joy of gardening

(D) How to plant vegetables

7. **Write three ideas that can be found in both passages.**

_____

_____

_____

_____

_____

_____

Name _____ Date _____

Use Nouns and Pronouns
Language

DIRECTIONS: Choose or write the correct answer.

> **Strategy**   Identify the noun in a sentence. Then, to make sure you use the correct noun, ask yourself if the noun is singular (one), plural (more than one), or possessive (belongs to).

> **Test Tip**   Some nouns change when they name more than one person, place, or thing. For example, child becomes children and mouse becomes mice.

1.Choose the sentence that is written correctly.

(A) My foots are so tired from walking!

(B) The childs played on the swings together.

(C) There were two mice under the stoop.

(D) Don't forget to brush your tooths.

2. Choose the sentence that is incorrect. Then, write it correctly.

(A) The children played at the park.

(B) I jumped more than two feet in the air!

(C) Caleb has lost three tooths already.

(D) Two mice ran across the field.

My correction:

_____

3. Write the sentence correctly on the line.

The knife go in that drawer.

_____

> # Test Tip
> A pronoun stands in for a noun. Some pronouns include *I, me, my, they, them, their, anyone, everything, myself, herself,* and *himself.* For singular nouns, use *he, she,* and *it.* For plural nouns, use *they* and *them.*

4. Choose the sentence that is written correctly.

(A) I gave myself a haircut!

(B) He got a new coat for hisself.

(C) I'm so excited, I can hardly control mineself.

(D) Yourself is really pretty.

5. Write the pronouns that replace the underlined words in the sentences.

Madelyn and Ryan study together.

Chris gave his math notes to Mike.

Sheri invited all of the students to the party.

_____

6. Choose the sentence that is incorrect. Then, write it correctly.

(A) Aubrey and Ben stayed home by themselves.

(B) Addison and William made themselves lunch.

(C) Addison poured herself some milk.

(D) John went by theirself to the store.

My correction:

_____

English Language Arts

Use Nouns and Pronouns
Language

Strategy | Use singular pronouns to replace singular nouns. Use plural pronouns to replace plural nouns.

Test Tip | Look up nouns in a dictionary to learn their plural form.

7. Write the plural form of each word on the line.

tooth _____

woman _____

fly _____

loaf _____

8. What do you call a group of

geese? _____

fish? _____

flowers? _____

cows? _____

9. Write the correct pronoun on the line.

He went to the store by _____.

10. Write a sentence using the pronouns below.

she herself

_____

_____

_____

11. Which nouns are replaced by the pronouns in the sentence below?

<u>They</u> built a fort all by <u>themselves</u>.

(A) Matt and Russ

(B) Boy

(C) Matt

(D) Russ

Write how you know.

_____

_____

_____

_____

English Language Arts

Use Verbs
Language

DIRECTIONS: Read each sentence and choose or write the correct answer.

Strategy | Use the endings of verbs to identify if the action is happening now, in the past, or in the future.

Test Tip | Verbs can show if an action is happening now, in the past, or in the future. This is called verb tense. Learn how to form each type of verb. Some past tense verbs change spelling.

Present	Past	Future
walks	walked	will walk
sits	sat	will sit
hides	hid	will hide

Test Tip

Read each sentence carefully to find verb errors. Try reading sentences out loud to yourself to hear how they sound.

1. Choose the sentence that is written correctly.

(A) I sitted on the bench.

(B) Jose set on the grass.

(C) Angel sat on the swing.

(D) Jesse sit on the slide.

2. Write the sentence using the past tense of hide.

The squirrel hides his nuts behind the tree.

_____

_____

3. Choose the sentence that uses a verb in the future tense.

(A) My mom tell me a funny story.

(B) I told it to Sue.

(C) Sue will tell it to Cate.

(D) Cate tolded it to Victor.

4. Choose the sentence that is written correctly.

(A) Last summer, I swum at the beach.

(B) Yesterday, I swimmed in a pool.

(C) Last week, Abbie swam in a lake.

(D) Sam swamed in a river.

5. Choose the sentence that is incorrect. Then, write it correctly.

(A) Marco hitted the ball very hard.

(B) Luke sat in the back seat.

(C) Hannah hid in the closet.

(D) Mr. Jones runs three miles.

My correction:

_____

6. Choose the sentence that is incorrect. Then, write it correctly.

(A) We ate at a nice restaurant yesterday.

(B) They eat at home on Tuesdays.

(C) I eat at school every day.

(D) Ethan eated at his friend's house last week.

My correction:

_____

_____

_____

Use Verbs
Language

DIRECTIONS: Read the sentence. Write the past tense of the verb correctly on the line.

Strategy Try the verb in different tenses in the sentences. Read the sentences to yourself to see which word makes sense.

Test Tip Remember that some verbs do not use *–ed* at the end when they are put into past tense. For example, the past tense of go is *went*. Some verbs don't change at all. The past tense of *let* is *let*.

7. Complete the chart with the correct verb tense.

Present	Past	Future
fly	flew	will fly
bend	bent	will bend
talk	talked	will talk
hop	hopped	will hop
see	saw	will see
snow	snowed	will snow

8. The dog _____ on the grass. (sit)

9. I _____ to the mall yesterday. (go)

10. It _____ to rain outside. (begin)

11. Sophie _____ her breath for 15 seconds! (hold)

12. Kevin _____ his leg playing soccer. (hurt)

13. Olivia _____ a new friend yesterday. (meet)

14. Isabella _____ a sticker on my paper. (put)

DIRECTIONS: Write a sentence that uses the past tense of the verb.

15. ride

Yesterday,

_____

16. say

Last night,

_____

17. dig

Last weekend,

_____

18. bite

Yesterday,

_____

English Language Arts

Use Adjectives and Adverbs
Language

DIRECTIONS: Read each sentence. Choose the word that fits best in the sentence.

Strategy | Identify the noun and verb in a sentence. Then, look for words that tell more about the noun (how it looks or sounds) and words that tell more about the verb (how the action is done).

Test Tip | Remember the difference between adjectives and adverbs to use them correctly. Adjectives tell more about nouns, or a person, place, or thing. Adverbs tell more about verbs, or an action.

1. I ran _____ to my bus stop.
- (A) quick
- (B) fastly
- (C) slow
- (D) quickly

2. The boat sailed _____ down the river.
- (A) peacefully
- (B) fast
- (C) slow
- (D) quick

Test Tip

Adjectives have endings such as *-ful, -less, -er,* and *-est.*

3. The _____ soldiers fought in the battle.
- (A) braves
- (B) bravely
- (C) braved
- (D) bravest

4. We walked by the _____ water.
- (A) peaceful
- (B) careful
- (C) slower
- (D) carefully

5. The _____ snow fell _____.
- (A) soundless, gently
- (B) some, quick
- (C) loud, hard
- (D) sits, sat

6. John walked _____ toward the door.
- (A) fastly
- (B) slower
- (C) quickly
- (D) sad

7. Sally sat _____ waiting for someone to speak first.
- (A) loud
- (B) silently
- (C) calm
- (D) hardly

Use Adjectives and Adverbs
Language

DIRECTIONS: Choose or write the correct answer.

Strategy Use the endings of words to identify if a word is an adjective or an adverb.

Test Tip The ending *-ly* usually means a word is an adverb. Use an adverb to describe how something is done.

DIRECTIONS: Read each sentence. Write a word on each line to complete the sentence.

8. I have _____ hair.

9. Liam has a _____ bike.

10. The _____ dog was barking _____ .

11. The _____ man walked _____ in the park.

12. **Read the words. Write the words in the correct box.**

    Words:

    quick   quickly   old   pretty   carefully   honest

    wet   slowly   softly   silly   lovely   sadly

Test Tip Use each word in a sentence to decide if it is an adjective or an adverb. Adjectives describe people, places, and things.

Adjectives	Adverbs

13. **Write three sentences using adjectives and adverbs.**

Test Tip Most adjectives come before the noun. Most adverbs come after the verb.

_____

_____

_____

_____

English Language Arts

Use Capitals and Punctuation
Language

DIRECTIONS: Choose or write the word in the sentence that needs to be capitalized.

Strategy | Identify words in a sentence that should be capitalized—the first word, proper nouns. Then, to figure out which end punctuation to use, ask yourself if the sentence is a statement or command, a question, or a sentence with feeling.

Test Tip | Sentences begin with capital letters. Holidays, product names, and geographic names begin with capital letters.

1. **Football practice will start on monday.**

   (A) Practice

   (B) Will

   (C) Start

   (D) Monday

2. **My friends will visit us on thanksgiving.**

   Write the word that needs a capital letter correctly on the line.

   _____

   Write how you know.

   _____

   _____

3. **Jake is going to the movie theater on elm street.**

   (A) Going

   (B) Movie Theater

   (C) On

   (D) Elm Street

4. **lily lived in mexico, but now she lives in the united states.**

   Write the sentence with correct capitalization.

   _____

   _____

DIRECTIONS: Read the sentence. Choose or write the correct contraction to replace the two underlined words.

Test Tip

Identify the two words that make up a contraction. Choose the word that has the apostrophe in the correct place.

5. **The phone is not ringing.**

   (A) isn't

   (B) is'nt

   (C) i'snt

   (D) isnt'

6. **It is very hot outside today.**

   (A) I'ts

   (B) Its'

   (C) It's

   (D) Its

7. **Rewrite this sentence replacing the underlined words with a contraction.**

   I do not like to swim in the ocean.

   _____

   _____

Use Capitals and Punctuation
Language

DIRECTIONS: Read each letter. Choose the sentence that is incorrect. Then, write the sentence correctly on the line.

Strategy | As you read each sentence, look for missing capitalization and missing punctuation.

Test Tip | Remember that the greeting and closing of a letter must include a comma.

8.

Dear Eva

    I hope you are having a good vacation. I love Greenville. It is beautiful here. I will see you on Spring Break.

        Love,

          Mary

(A) Dear Eva

(B) I hope you are having a good vacation.

(C) I love Greenville.

(D) Love, Mary

_____

_____

9. **Marissa went to ohio to go shopping. She bought a pretty dress. Then, she went to a restaurant on Main Street for lunch. She ate a grilled cheese sandwich.**

(A) Marissa went to ohio to go shopping.

(B) She bought a pretty dress.

(C) Then, she went to a restaurant on Main Street for lunch.

(D) She ate a grilled cheese sandwich.

_____

_____

10. **Next week is Halloween. Mason and I are dressing alike. Were going to make monster costumes. I think we are going to have lots of fun!**

(A) Next week is Halloween.

(B) Mason and I are dressing alike.

(C) Were going to make monster costumes.

(D) I think we are going to have lots of fun!

_____

11. **Write the letter below using correct capitalization and punctuation. Write the letter on the lines.**

Dear Zoe

    I hope you can come to my party It will be at harborside Park. It starts at 2:00. We will have cake and ice cream

Your Friend

Chloe

_____

_____

_____

_____

_____

_____

_____

_____

Determine Word Meanings
Language

DIRECTIONS: Read each short paragraph. Choose or write the best word to answer each question.

Strategy | Use context clues, prefixes, root words, and smaller word parts to help you choose the meaning of words.

Test Tip | When choosing the best answer, try each answer choice in the blank.

The _____ was easy to enter. All you had to do was go to the park. To win, you had to _____ how many jelly beans were in the jar.

1. What word should go in the first blank?

- (A) door
- (B) contest
- (C) tunnel
- (D) house

2. What word should go in the second blank?

- (A) guess
- (B) read
- (C) count
- (D) sing

Each house on the block had a _____ backyard. Each had small patches of lawn and flowers. Some even had _____ gardens.

3. What word should go in the first blank?

- (A) unlikely
- (B) neat
- (C) lost
- (D) firm

4. What word should go in the second blank?

- (A) sand
- (B) problem
- (C) vegetable
- (D) blanket

Test Tip

If you know that *un-* means "not," you can find the meaning of the word *unhappy*.

5. Mia was very unhappy because her dog was sick. What does *unhappy* mean?

- (A) not angry
- (B) happy again
- (C) not happy
- (D) excited again

6. Write the meaning of *retell* on the line.

Please retell your story to the class.

_____

Test Tip

Two words that make one new word are compound words. Make sure each part is a word on its own.

7. Write the two words that make up the compound word lighthouse.

_____

8. What word has the same root as *bicycle*?

- (A) biweekly
- (B) recycle
- (C) binoculars
- (D) billion

Determine Word Meaning
Language

DIRECTIONS: Put two words or word parts together to make a new word that matches the definition. Each word or word part can be used more than once.

> ## Strategy
> Use the meanings of prefixes and root words to make new words and define words.

> ## Test Tip
> Try different words and word parts together to see what words you can make.

happy	bird	shelf	house
un	dis	like	cage

9. a place for a bird to live _____

10. not happy _____

11. a feeling of not liking someone or something

_____

un	re	tell	read
lock	tie	sun	rain
bow	shine	foot	fire
camp	ball		

12. read again _____

13. open with a key _____

14. the light outside during the day _____

15. make your shoe not tied _____

16. a colorful line in the sky after a rain shower

_____

17. where you roast marshmallows

_____

18. tell again _____

19. a short necktie tied in a bowknot _____

20. Use two of the words you made in a sentence.

_____

_____

_____

_____

English Language Arts

Determine Shades of Meaning
Language

DIRECTIONS: Order the words in the chart according to their strength.

Strategy Compare words that have similar meanings by asking which word has a stronger meaning. Then, choose the word that fits in the sentence.

Test Tip Some words may seem similar, but they really have different meanings. For example, *hold* and *grab* mean about the same thing. But *hold* makes you think of gently holding something. *Grab* makes you think of holding on tightly.

EXAMPLE

Not Strong	A Little Strong	Strong
big	large	gigantic
jog	run	dash

1.
thin	good	okay	call
skinny	happy	warm	crabby
furious	yell	hurl	scrawny
excellent	toss	hot	angry
thrilled	boiling	cool	shout
cold	throw	pleased	freezing

Not Strong	A Little Strong	Strong
thin	skinny	scrawny
toss	throw	hurl
okay	good	excellent
warm	hot	boiling
cool	cold	freezing
crabby	angry	furious
call	yell	shout
pleased	happy	thrilled

2. **Choose the sentences with the underlined word that uses the correct strength of meaning. Choose all that apply.**

   Ⓐ The tiny kitten was so <u>skinny</u> he fit in my hand.

   Ⓑ The snowy, icy day was <u>cool</u>, so I wore a scarf and hat.

   Ⓒ Dan yelled <u>loudly</u> to the woman who hit his car.

   Ⓓ She was <u>thrilled</u> when she found a penny on the road.

3. **What happens if a sentence uses a word that has too strong of a meaning?**

   _____

   _____

   _____

   _____

   _____

   _____

   _____

English Language Arts

Determine Shades of Meaning
Language

DIRECTIONS: Read each sentence. Write the word that best fits on the line.

Strategy — Use other words in the sentence to help you choose the word with the best meaning.

1. The air was _____, so I put on a long-sleeved shirt.

    cool   cold   freezing

2. Be careful! The water on the stove is

    _____!

    warm   hot   boiling

Test Tip

While you read, picture the word in your mind to see how strong the word is. Choose the word that matches the meaning of the sentence.

3. I was late for school, so I _____ as fast as I could.

    jogged   ran   sprinted

4. The temperature is -20°F. It is _____ outside.

    cool   cold   freezing

5. I _____ quickly in the mirror as I dashed out the door.

    glanced   looked   stared

DIRECTIONS: Read each sentence. Rewrite the sentence by replacing the underlined word or words with a word that is stronger.

6. Ella is <u>angry</u> today.

    _____

    _____

7. I <u>don't like</u> Brussels sprouts, but I will eat them if it means getting dessert!

    _____

    _____

    _____

8. We got <u>wet</u> on the boat ride at the amusement park!

    _____

    _____

9. I could see steam from the <u>warm</u> cup of tea.

    _____

    _____

10. She was <u>pleased</u> to win first prize in the contest!

    _____

    _____

English Language Arts

Write an Opinion
Writing

Strategy Plan your writing by stating your opinion and listing reasons you have that opinion. Then, begin writing. When you are finished writing, read your paragraph to yourself. Make sure you included everything listed in the directions. Make sure your writing is clear and fix any errors.

DIRECTIONS: An opinion paragraph tells how you feel about a topic. It gives reasons why you feel that way. Write an opinion paragraph about your favorite place in your town.

Your paragraph should have:

- A sentence to introduce your topic
- A statement of your opinion
- Some reasons for your opinion
- Linking words to connect your opinion and reasons
- A sentence to end your paragraph

Read the example paragraph to see how one student wrote an opinion paragraph about his favorite food.

EXAMPLE

My favorite food is tacos. I like tacos because they are crunchy and spicy. I like to eat my tacos with sour cream and hot sauce. My favorite part of eating tacos is tasting the spicy, delicious meat with the cool, crisp toppings. I think tacos are the best food.

Test Tip A good way to check spelling and punctuation is to read your paragraph backward, from the end to the beginning.

_____

_____

_____

_____

_____

_____

_____

_____

_____

Write an Opinion
Writing

DIRECTIONS: An opinion paragraph tells how you feel about a topic. It gives reasons why you feel that way. Write an opinion paragraph about your favorite animal.

Your paragraph should have:

- A sentence to introduce your topic
- A statement of your opinion
- Some reasons for your opinion
- Linking words to connect your opinion and reasons
- A sentence to end your paragraph

Read the example paragraph to see how one student wrote an opinion paragraph about her favorite book.

> **EXAMPLE**
>
> My favorite book is *Island of the Blue Dolphins.* I like this book because the main character is a very strong girl. The book is interesting because Karana gets stranded on an island. She is very brave and survives for many years by herself. My favorite thing about this book is that it is based on a true story. I think that *Island of the Blue Dolphins* is a wonderful book.

_____

_____

_____

_____

_____

_____

_____

_____

_____

_____

English Language Arts

Write an Informative Paragraph
Writing

Strategy Plan your writing by listing details that relate to your topic or main idea. Then, begin writing. When you are finished writing, read your paragraph to yourself. Make sure you included everything listed in the directions. Make sure your writing is clear and fix any errors.

DIRECTIONS: An informative paragraph gives facts about a topic. Use what you already know and the facts below to write an informative paragraph about the habitat of a specific animal.

Your paragraph should have:

- A topic sentence
- Facts and definitions to develop your points
- A sentence or section to end your paragraph

Animal Habitat Facts
- a special place where an animal lives
- must give animals 5 things: food, shelter, water, air, safety
- can be big or small
- different habitats for different animals
- some animals share with other animals
- some compete with other animals

Test Tip Put a mark next to the facts you want to use in your paragraph. Organize the facts you chose so that your paragraph makes sense. Then, add details to each fact to make your writing more interesting.

Use this space to plan your paragraph.

_____

_____

_____

_____

_____

_____

_____

English Language Arts

Write an Informative Paragraph
Writing

DIRECTIONS: Write your informative paragraph. When you finish, use the checklist below.

Checklist:

☐ I have a clear topic sentence.

☐ I have details that support my topic.

☐ I used nouns correctly.

☐ I used pronouns correctly.

☐ I used verbs correctly.

☐ I used adjectives and adverbs to make my writing interesting.

English Language Arts

Write an Explanatory Paragraph
Writing

Strategy   After you choose a topic, plan your writing by making a list of the steps.

DIRECTIONS: An explanatory paragraph can give directions for doing something. Choose a topic from the list. Write an explanatory paragraph telling how to do it.

Your paragraph should have:

- A topic sentence
- Clear steps to follow
- Facts and definitions to support your details
- A sentence or section to end your paragraph

Topics
- **How to make a sandwich (you pick what kind!)**
- **How to make a bed**
- **How to wash a dog**
- **How to play a game (you pick the game!)**
- **How to get ready for school**
- **How to brush your teeth**
- **How to do something else that you are an expert at**

Use this space to plan your paragraph. Write the steps you need to follow. Add details that the reader should know.

_____

_____

_____

_____

_____

_____

_____

_____

_____

_____

Name _____ Date _____

Write an Explanatory Paragraph
Writing

DIRECTIONS: Write your explanatory paragraph. When you finish, use the checklist below.

Test Tip   Use words like *first, next, then,* and *finally* to show the order of steps to follow.

Checklist:

- ☐ I have a clear topic sentence.
- ☐ I have clear steps to follow.
- ☐ I have facts and definitions that support my topic.
- ☐ I used nouns correctly.
- ☐ I used pronouns correctly.
- ☐ I used verbs correctly.
- ☐ I used adjectives and adverbs to make my writing interesting.

Write a Narrative
Writing

Strategy Plan a narrative by choosing people, places, and events that will be in the story. Remember that a story should have a beginning, middle, and end.

DIRECTIONS: A narrative is a story. Narratives can be about real events or imaginary events. Answer the questions below and use them to write a narrative about an event in your life.

Your narrative should have:

- Details to describe your thoughts, actions, and feelings
- Interesting details about what happened
- Time words like *first, next, then,* and *finally*
- Adjectives to describe people, things, and events
- An ending sentence

Strategy Organize details in a web to help you decide which details are important to use and which ones you can skip.

Use the Graphic Organizer to plan your narrative. Write the name of the event in the center circle. Write details about the event in the outer circles. Describe what you saw. Describe how you felt. Describe what you heard or smelled. Describe who was there. Add circles if you need more.

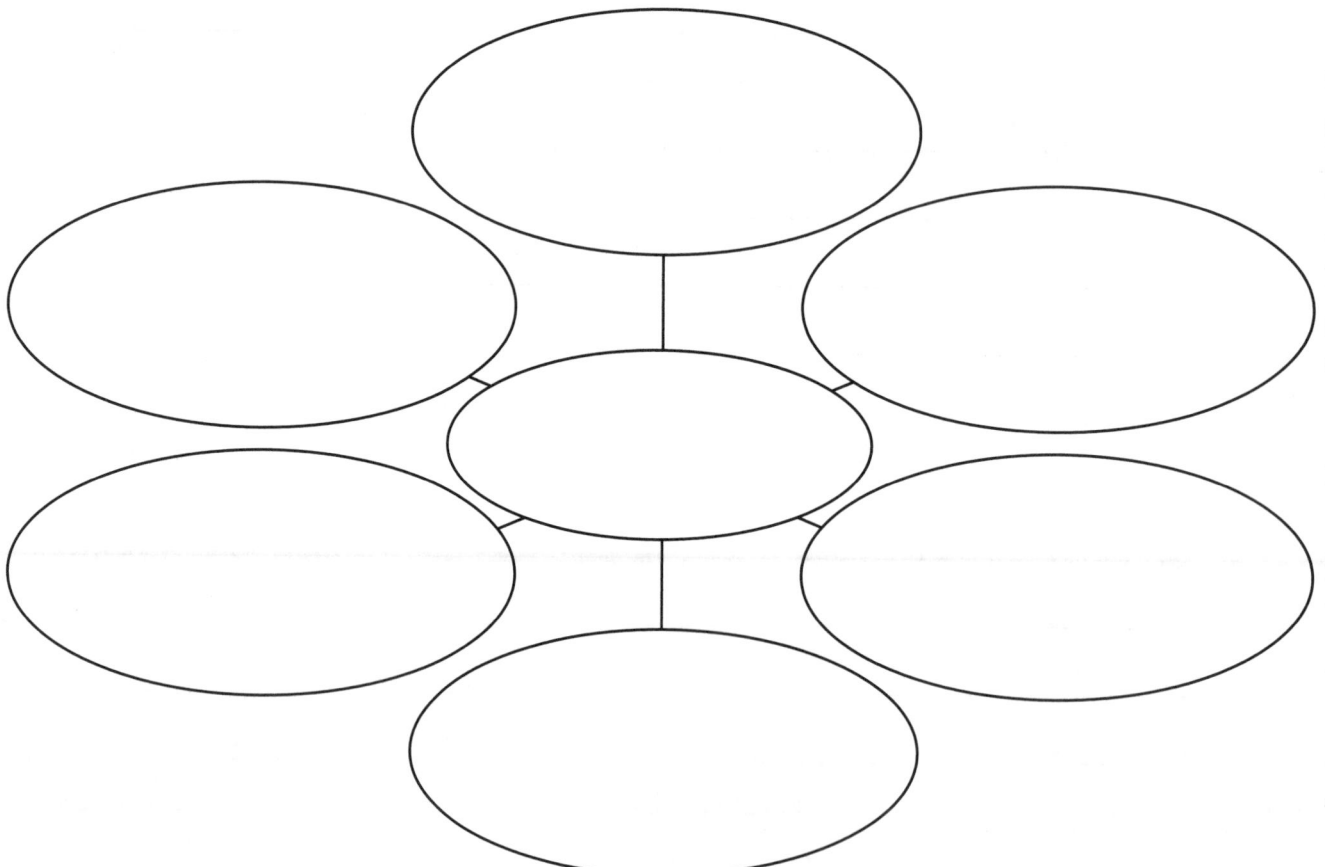

English Language Arts

Write a Narrative
Writing

DIRECTIONS: Write your narrative. When you finish, use the checklist below.

> **Test Tip**   Use the checklist below to make sure you have everything in your paragraph.

Checklist

☐ I wrote about an event that happened in my life.

☐ I have clear details that tell about the event.

☐ I included details about my thoughts, feelings, and actions.

☐ I used pronouns correctly.

☐ I have a satisfying ending.

_____

_____

_____

_____

_____

_____

_____

_____

_____

_____

_____

_____

_____

_____

_____

_____

_____

Strategy Review

In this section, you will review the strategies you learned and apply them to practice the skills.

Strategy | Use details from a story or passage to show your understanding.

It was a rainy afternoon. Ty sat in his house watching the rain slide down the front window. His sister was taking a nap. His mom was cleaning the kitchen. Ty didn't know what to do. There was nothing on TV. The computer was broken. He got up and wandered to the basement. There were boxes and stacks of paper, old books, and photo albums. Ty wandered and peeked in boxes. An hour later, his mom called him. He ran upstairs.

"What have you been doing in that dirty basement?" his mom asked.

Ty pulled on his mom's hand. "Come and see, Mom," he said. They went down the stairs. Ty led his mom through the maze of old junk. Finally, he stopped. His mom looked at the giant cardboard robot in front of her.

"Oh, my!" she said. "You have been very busy."

First, read the story. Think about what a rainy day is like.

Next, make a connection. What do you like to do on rainy days?

Finally, read the questions that go with the story. Think about what you read or look back at the story. You can pick out key words in the question and look for those words in the story to find the answer quickly.

1. Why was Ty looking for something to do?

Ⓐ He was home sick from school.

Ⓑ It was snowing and he couldn't go outside.

Ⓒ The TV was broken.

Ⓓ It was raining and he had nothing to do.

2. How did Ty solve his problem?

_____

Read the next story about a rainy day. Think about how it is the same as the story you just read. Think about how it is different.

Jess flipped on the TV. Nothing. She picked up a book and started reading. She just couldn't get into the story. Finally, Jess went upstairs to her bedroom.

Jess looked around her room for something to do. Suddenly, she spotted the new art set her aunt had bought her for her last birthday.

"Well," thought Jess, "it's something to do."

Jess opened the art set and began creating. When her mom called at lunchtime, Jess ran to the phone.

"I'm fine, Mom," she answered. "But, I can't talk right now. I'm really busy."

3. Why was Jess looking for something to do?

_____

Jess was home alone. Mom and Dad were at work. She didn't usually mind being alone, but today she was bored.

"There's nothing to do!" she complained to her dog, Sally.

Sally looked at Jess, but said nothing.

"You're no help," Jess said, patting the beagle's brown head.

4. Write how the two stories are alike.

_____

_____

_____

English Language Arts

Strategy Review

Strategy | While reading, look carefully at pictures to help you better understand the story or passage.

When you read stories or informational text, there are often pictures, too. The pictures are there to help you understand the words better. An author carefully chooses pictures that will support the main idea of the story or passage.

Read the passage and look at the picture. Then, answer the questions.

Changing Phones

Technology changes quickly. One form of technology that has changed a lot since it was first invented is the telephone. When Alexander Graham Bell invented the first telephone in 1876, he shaped it like a metal cone. It had a thin piece of paper stretched like a drum over one end. A cork with a needle stuck in it was glued to the outside of the paper.

Phones have changed greatly from that first model. For decades, most people have had at least one phone in their home. The first phones had a separate earpiece and mouthpiece. Then, the two were combined into one. Early home phones were hard-wired into the home. You could not talk on the phone if you weren't connected to the wall! Later, cordless phones were invented. Finally, you could call your friend and wander throughout the house chatting. But, you still could not go very far away from the phone's base.

The first mobile phone was invented in 1973. The handset weighed 2.2 pounds! The cell phones most people have today have evolved from that first mobile phone. Who knows what the future will bring?

First, read the passage and make connections to the details. How are the phones mentioned in the story alike? How are they different?

Next, study the picture. Ask yourself how the picture adds details that are not in the passage.

Finally, read the questions that go with the passage. Use the picture and details from the passage to help you answer the questions.

1. **Write what one model of the telephone looked like.**

_____

_____

How did the strategy help you answer these questions?

_____

2. **Choose two ways the phone in the picture is different from the first phone.**

Ⓐ The first phone was shaped like a donut.

Ⓑ The first phone was shaped like a cone.

Ⓒ The first phone did not have a handset.

Ⓓ The first phone could be used anywhere.

Strategy Review

STRATEGIES

- Look for connecting words like *because* and *so* to understand why something happens in a passage.

- Look for words that explain the meaning of new words. Looking for commas or the keyword can help you find these words.

- Plan your writing.

- When you write, use details to support main ideas.

EXAMPLE

Sabrina likes to go <u>spelunking</u>, or exploring caves, on weekends.
What is spelunking?
First, look for the new word.
Sabrina likes to go <u>spelunking</u>, or exploring caves, on weekends.
Next, look for the keyword *or* and commas.
Sabrina likes to go spelunking, <u>or exploring caves,</u> on weekends.
Spelunking means exploring caves.

Choose the part of the sentence that answers the question.

1. **Adam is using crutches because he sprained his ankle in a soccer game. Why is Adam using crutches?**

   (A) Adam is

   (B) using crutches

   (C) because he sprained his ankle

   (D) in a soccer game

2. **Abe likes to eat latkes, fried potato pancakes, when he goes to his aunt's house for Passover. What are latkes?**

   (A) Abe likes to eat latkes

   (B) fried potato pancakes

   (C) when he goes to his aunt's house

   (D) for Passover

Example

Write a paragraph that tells how to brush your teeth.

Start by planning your paragraph.

First, list the steps you must follow.

1. get toothbrush and toothpaste

2. put toothpaste on the toothbrush

3. rub the toothpaste into your teeth for 2 minutes

4. rinse the toothpaste out of your mouth

5. clean off your toothbrush

Then, add details and write your paragraph.

There are important steps to brushing your teeth. First, you will need a toothbrush and toothpaste. Squeeze toothpaste onto the toothbrush. Then, rub the toothpaste into your teeth. Brush all of your teeth on all sides. Do this for two minutes. Next, rinse the toothpaste out of your mouth with water. Finally, clean your toothbrush so it is ready for next time.

3. **Write a paragraph about how to eat a bowl of cereal. First, plan your paragraph by writing the steps of eating cereal.**

   1. _____

   2. _____

   3. _____

4. **Add details and write your paragraph on the lines.**

   _____

   _____

   _____

   _____

Strategy Review

Write a story about getting ready for school.

This morning I got up early for school. First, I took a shower and brushed my teeth. Next, I dressed in nice, warm clothes. After that, I dried and combed my hair. I ate breakfast and then had to brush my teeth again! Finally, I put on my coat and hat, grabbed my backpack, and headed to the bus stop.

1. **Write a short story about visiting a zoo, park, or museum. First, plan your paragraph by writing the events in order from first to last.**

_____

_____

_____

_____

_____

_____

2. **Add details and write your paragraph on the lines.**

_____

_____

_____

_____

_____

_____

Strategy Revise to make sure your writing makes sense. Then, edit to fix errors.

After you write your first draft, you should read it over. Read the story out loud to yourself to make sure it makes sense. Look for places where the reader might have trouble understanding what you wanted to say. Look for words that need capitals. Look for places that need punctuation marks. Finally, look for words that might be spelled wrong.

Strategies for Mathematics Tests

Read the strategies below to learn more about how they work.

Use basic operations to solve problems.

You can use what you know about adding, subtracting, multiplying, and dividing to solve many different types of problems. Make sure you know your basic math facts. This will save time on the test and make sure your answers are correct.

Use graphs, tables, and drawings to understand data.

Sometimes, making a drawing of a word problem helps you figure out how to solve it. Other times, making a graph or line plot is a way to show numbers or amounts of something. Drawings, number lines, line plots, and other graphs all use numbers.

Read word problems carefully. Make sure you know what you are asked to do.

Whenever you need to solve a word problem, you should first ask *What information do I know?* Then, you should ask *What question am I being asked to answer?* or *What am I being asked to find?* Don't start solving until you know the answers to these questions!

Choose the right tool and units to measure objects.

Certain tools are used to measure length, weight, and temperature. Remember that measurements all have units. Lengths are often measured in inches (in.), feet (ft), centimeters (cm), or meters (m). Weight is often measured in pounds (lb), grams (g), or kilograms (kg). Temperature can be measured in degrees Celsius (°C) or degrees Fahrenheit (°F).

Use what you know about numbers, shapes, and measurement to answer questions.

Using what you already know about numbers, shapes, and measurement, you can answer many different types of questions.

Math

Solve One-Step Problems: Add and Subtract
Numbers and Operations

DIRECTIONS: Choose the best answer.

EXAMPLE

30 cows are in the field. 15 cows are in the barn. Write a number sentence that you can use to find how many cows there are in all. Use a ☐ for the number of cows in all.

_____ ☐ _____ = ☐

Answer: 30 + 15 = ☐

Solve your number sentence and tell how many cows there are in all.

30 + 15 = ☐

Answer: 30 + 15 = 45; There are 45 cows in all.

Strategy | Use drawings, number sentences, and basic facts to solve word problems.

Test Tip | First, think about what question is being asked in the problem. Then, decide if you need to add or subtract.

1. There are 49 ants in Lila's ant farm. Lila bought more ants to put in the ant farm. There are now 67 ants in her ant farm. Write a number sentence that you can use to find how many ants Lila bought. The ☐ stands for the number of ants Lila bought.

_____ – _____ = ☐

How did you find your answer?

_____

_____

_____

Test Tip

Words like *how much farther, how many were left*, and *how much more* usually mean you will need to subtract.

2. Cheri and Katrina were having a baseball throwing contest. Cheri threw the baseball 56 feet. Katrina threw the ball 68 feet. How much farther did Katrina throw the ball than Cheri? Explain how you found your answer.

_____

_____

_____

_____

_____

3. Kia had some math problems to do for homework. She did 5 problems. There were 10 problems still left to do. Which number sentences show this situation? Choose all that apply.

(A) 15 – 5 = 10

(B) 10 – 5 = 5

(C) 15 + 5 = 20

(D) 5 + 10 = 15

Solve One-Step Problems: Add and Subtract
Numbers and Operations

DIRECTIONS: Choose the best answer.

Strategy   Draw the number of objects in a word problem and find clue words that tell if you are adding or subtracting. Then, use the picture and clue words to write a number sentence.

Test Tip   Words like *in all, all together,* and *total* usually mean you will need to add.

4. Lisa practiced the violin for 35 minutes on Monday and 46 minutes on Wednesday. Which number sentence shows how many minutes in all Lisa practiced on Monday and Wednesday?

    Ⓐ 35 + 46 = 81

    Ⓑ 46 − 35 = 11

    Ⓒ 11 + 35 = 66

    Ⓓ 81 + 35 = 116

5. Dara's grandmother is 48 years old. Her grandfather is 51 years old. Which number sentence shows how much older Dara's grandfather is than Dara's grandmother?

    Ⓐ 48 + 51 = 99

    Ⓑ 51 − 48 = 3

    Ⓒ 48 + 3 = 51

    Ⓓ 99 − 51 = 48

Write how you know.

_____

_____

6. Felipe has 17 nickels in his coin bank. His dad gave him 8 more nickels to put in his bank. How many nickels does Felipe have in his coin bank now? Draw a picture and write a number sentence to show how you found your answer.

7. Sandra wants to make a quilt using a total of 19 green and yellow squares of cloth. She can use any number of green and yellow squares as long as they total 19. How many yellow squares and how many green squares could Sandra use to make her quilt? Use words, numbers, or pictures to show how you found your answer.

8. Mandy's uncle has 12 horses on his farm. He has 17 more cows than horses. Write a number sentence that shows how many cows Mandy's uncle has.

_____

Now, solve the problem.

_____

Solve Two-Step Problems: Add and Subtract
Numbers and Operations

DIRECTIONS: Choose or write the correct answer.

Strategy

Use clue words and basic addition and subtraction facts to solve problems. First, think about what question is being asked in the problem. Then, decide if you need to add or subtract, or do both operations.

Test Tip

A number sentence includes symbols such as +, –, and =.

EXAMPLE

Luisa picked some berries. She put 50 strawberries in a basket. Then, she ate 15 of the berries before picking 11 more. Write a number sentence that you can use to find how many berries are left in the basket. Use a ☐ for the number of berries left.

Answer: 50 – 15 + 11 = ☐

Solve your number sentence.

Answer: 50 – 15 + 11 = 46

1. Jeff and his family are going to his uncle's house. They drive 45 minutes. Jeff's dad spends another 12 minutes getting gas and 5 minutes waiting in traffic. How long does it take the family to make the trip? Write a number sentence that you can use to find how long the trip takes. Use a ☐ for the unknown number.

_____

Solve your number sentence and tell how long it takes the family to make the trip.

_____

2. At the county fair, Jamal wants to go on 8 rides and play 5 games. When he gets there, he decides not to go on 2 of the rides. How many activities did Jamal do all together at the county fair? Show how you got your answer.

3. Leesa has 20 math problems for homework. She does 5 problems after school and 4 more problems after piano practice. How many problems does Leesa have left to do? Which number sentence shows this situation? Choose all that apply.

(A) 20 – 5 – 4 = 11
(B) 20 – 5 + 4 = 19
(C) 20 – 4 – 5 = 11
(D) 20 – 5 + 4 = 19

4. Tomas has 10 balls and 3 bats. He gives Kiley 4 balls. Then, he gives Carlo 1 bat. Which number sentence can you use to find how many balls and bats in all Tomas has left? Choose all that apply.

(A) 10 + 3 – 4 – 1 = ☐
(B) 13 – 4 – 1 = ☐
(C) 10 + 3 – 5 = ☐
(D) 10 – 3 + 5 – 4 = ☐

5. Angela wrote this number sentence to solve a problem.

10 – 8 + ☐ = 9

Write a word problem that Angela might have solved.

Math

Solve Two-Step Problems: Add and Subtract
Numbers and Operations

Strategy — Read the questions in word problems carefully. Underline words that are clues to adding or subtracting. Then, identify the order of operations—should you add or subtract first?

Test Tip — Words like *how many in all* and *how many all together* usually mean you will need to add.

6. Camilo has 13 dimes in his coin bank. His dad gives him 6 more dimes to put in his bank. Then, Felipe takes out 4 dimes to buy some pencils. How many dimes does Felipe have in his coin bank now? Use numbers or pictures to show how you found your answer.

7. Ana is making a picture using 3 different colors of paper squares. She uses a total of 16 squares. Some of the squares are orange, 5 are yellow, and 8 are green. How many squares of paper are orange? Choose the best answer.

(A) 3

(B) 8

(C) 11

(D) 13

8. Dora is 7 years old. Her brother is 8 years older than her. Dora's sister is 3 years older than her brother. What are the ages of Dora's brother and sister? Write how you know.

_____

_____

_____

_____

_____

9. Sheri and Paolo each bought a peach for 15 cents. Lian bought an apple for 5 cents more than a peach. How much did they spend all together for the fruit? Write in the blanks to make a number sentence. Then, solve it.

_____ + _____ + 15 + _____ = □

_____

10. Meg and Yolanda had 18 buckets of sand all together. Meg used 8 buckets of sand to build a sand castle. Yolanda used the same amount of sand to build her castle. Which number sentence shows how much sand was NOT used by the girls? Choose the best answer.

(A) 18 + 8 = 16

(B) 18 − 8 − 8 = 2

(C) 18 + 8 − 8 = 18

(D) 18 − 8 = 10

Write another number sentence that can be used to solve the problem. Write how you know.

_____

_____

_____

_____

_____

_____

Math

Use Mental Math: Add and Subtract Within 20
Numbers and Operations

DIRECTIONS: Choose or write the correct answer.

Strategy | Use addition and subtraction facts to solve word problems. For example, if you know the addition fact 8 + 4 = 12 you can write subtraction facts: 12 − 8 = 4 or 12 − 4 = 8.

Test Tip | Remember that a sum is the result of adding, and a difference is the result of subtracting.

EXAMPLE

Which two numbers have a sum of 9?

(A) 6 and 2

(B) 3 and 6

(C) 9 and 1

(D) 4 and 6

Answer: B

3 + 6 = 9

1. **Which have a sum or difference of 4? Choose all that apply.**

   (A) 7 + 3

   (B) 9 − 6

   (C) 2 + 2

   (D) 8 − 4

2. **There are 14 children in the room. 8 of them are girls. How many are boys? Write how you know.**

   _____

   _____

   _____

3. **Lin knows that 6 + 9 = 15. Write in the blanks to show two related subtraction facts Lin can write.**

   _____ − _____ = _____

   _____ − _____ = _____

4. **Mark isn't sure of the sum of 6 + 7. How can Mark use the doubles fact 6 + 6 = 12 to find the sum of 6 + 7?**

   _____

   _____

   _____

Test Tip

You can draw a picture to help you find the combination of nickels and dimes that make 6 coins in all.

5. **Josie has 6 coins in her bank. They are nickels and dimes. She says she has 4 dimes and 4 nickels. Can this be true? Tell why or why not.**

   _____

   _____

   _____

   How many nickels and how many dimes can Josie have in her bank? Write three possibilities.

   _____

   _____

   _____

Math
Use Mental Math: Add and Subtract Within 20
Numbers and Operations

Strategy | Write an addition or a subtraction sentence for a word problem. Then, reread the question to find out if you need a sum or a difference. Use your number sentence to solve the problem.

6. Solve each number sentence.

$3 + 3 =$ _____

$7 - 4 =$ _____

$16 - 8 =$ _____

$5 + 2 =$ _____

$8 + 3 =$ _____

7. Kyle has 14 picture books. He gives Siri 5 books to read. How many books does Kyle have left? Choose the best answer.

(A) 5

(B) 8

(C) 9

(D) 14

8. Write in the blank if the problem is true or false.

$6 + 2 = 8$ _____

$9 - 6 = 2$ _____

$8 + 3 = 11$ _____

$12 - 4 = 9$ _____

For each problem above that is false, write the correct sum or difference.

_____

9. Write two related addition facts for this subtraction fact: $17 - 9 = 8$

_____

_____

10. Write one related subtraction fact for this addition fact: $4 + 8 = 12$.

_____

11. Choose two addition and subtraction facts that are related.

(A) $7 + 4 = 11$

(B) $7 - 4 = 11$

(C) $11 - 4 = 7$

(D) $11 - 7 = 7$

Test Tip

Try each answer choice first. Find one choice that makes both number sentences true.

12. Write the missing number that solves both number sentences.

$5 + 7 =$ ☐

☐ $- 5 = 7$

Identify Odd and Even Numbers
Numbers and Operations

DIRECTIONS: Choose or write the correct answer.

Strategy
To identify odd and even numbers, look at the last digit of the number. If the digit is 0, 2, 4, 6, or 8, the number is even. If the last digit is 1, 3, 5, 7, or 9, the number is odd.

Test Tip
An *even* number is an amount that can be made of two equal parts with no leftovers. An *odd* number is one that that cannot be made of equal parts.

EXAMPLE

Which number is an odd number? Choose all that apply.

(A) 11

(B) 16

(C) 15

(D) 7

Answer: A, C, D

1. **Which group of numbers has three even numbers?**

   (A) 2, 8, 13, 15, 17, 20

   (B) 5, 8, 13, 14, 17, 19

   (C) 1, 3, 10, 15, 17, 19

   (D) 2, 7, 11, 12, 13, 19

2. **Gina says that the number 12 is an even number. Is she correct? Show how you know. Use words, numbers, or pictures.**

3. **Draw a circle around pairs of flowers. Then, tell if there are an odd or even number of flowers.**

_____

_____

_____

How many flowers are there?

_____

4. **Write odd or even on the line next to each picture.**

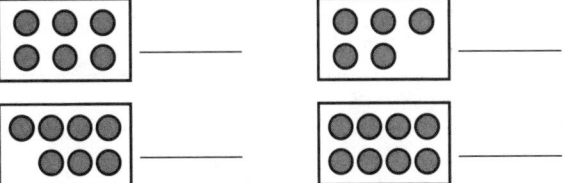

5. **Write odd or even on the line next to each number.**

   1 _____   10 _____

   12 _____   5 _____

   8 _____   17 _____

Identify Odd and Even Numbers
Numbers and Operations

Strategy Draw two columns of boxes for each number in a problem. Even numbers will have an equal number of boxes in each column. Odd numbers will have a column with one extra box.

6. **Which number sentence shows that 10 is an even number? Choose the best answer.**

   (A) 5 + 5 = 10

   (B) 3 + 7 = 10

   (C) 9 + 1 =10

   (D) 6 + 4 = 10

   Write how you know.

   _____

   _____

   _____

   _____

7. **Sasha says 6 is an even number. She drew this picture to prove her statement. How does this picture show that Sasha is correct?**

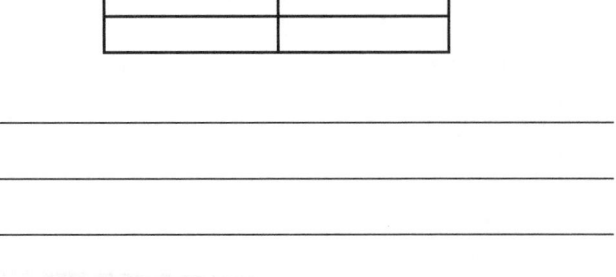

   _____

   _____

   _____

   _____

Test Tip

When more than one answer may be correct, read all choices and choose those that answer the question.

8. **There are 9 ants in a line. How many more ants are needed to make an even number of ants? Choose all that apply.**

   (A)

   (B)

   (C)

   (D)

Name _____ Date _____

Math

Use Arrays to Add
Numbers and Operations

DIRECTIONS: Choose or write the correct answer.

Strategy | Use addition to find the total number of objects arranged in rectangular arrays.

Test Tip | First, look at the picture and think of a number sentence to match the picture. Then, look at the answer choices to find a number sentence the same as your own.

EXAMPLE

What is the total number of dots? Write how you know.

○ ○ ○ ○ ○
○ ○ ○ ○ ○
○ ○ ○ ○ ○

There are 3 rows, with 5 dots in each row, so I can add 5 + 5 + 5 = 15.

There are 15 dots.

There are 5 columns, with 3 dots in each, so I can add 3 + 3 + 3 + 3 + 3 = 15.

There are 15 dots.

1. **Which number sentence can be used to find the total number of butterflies? Choose the best answer.**

Ⓐ 3 + 3 + 3 = ☐

Ⓑ 3 + 4 = ☐

Ⓒ 3 + 3 + 3 + 3 = ☐

Ⓓ 4 + 4 = ☐

2. **Akio planted her flowers in rows. How many flowers did Akio plant? Write how you know.**

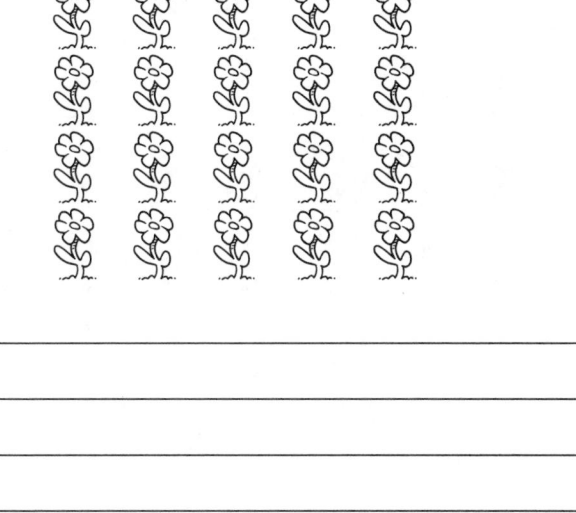

_____

_____

_____

_____

_____

3. **Fill in the blanks to write two number sentences that can be used to find how many paper clips in all.**

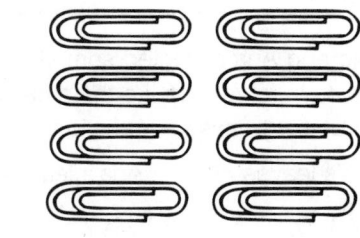

_____ + _____ + _____ + _____ = _____

_____ + _____ = _____

Use Arrays to Add
Numbers and Operations

Strategy   Use the pictures or draw your own pictures to understand arrays.

4. David wants to count his pennies. He places them in rows as shown below.

   Choose numbers from the box to complete the number sentences to find how many pennies David has. You may use each number more than once.

| 2 | 3 | 5 | 7 | 10 | 9 | 10 | 12 | 14 | 20 | 25 |

_____ + _____ + _____ = _____

_____ + _____ + _____ + _____ +

_____ + _____ + _____ = _____

5. Write an addition sentence to show the number of leaves that Julio has.

   _____

6. Write an addition sentence to show the number of leaves that Ana has.

   _____

7. Ana wants her array of leaves to look like Julio's. What does Ana need to do? Use words, numbers, or pictures to show your answer.

Test Tip

You can add the rows or the columns and get the same answer.

DIRECTIONS: Julio and Ana collected some leaves. They placed their leaves in rows to make them easier to count. Use the picture below to answer questions 5–7.

Julio's leaves   Ana's leaves

   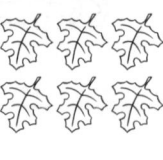

Name _____ Date _____

Math

Understand Place Value: Hundreds, Tens, Ones
Number and Operations

Strategy — Use place value to write and identify three-digit numbers. For example, use place value to write 5 hundreds, 2 tens, and 4 ones as 524.

DIRECTIONS: Choose or write the correct answer.

EXAMPLE

What number do the blocks represent?

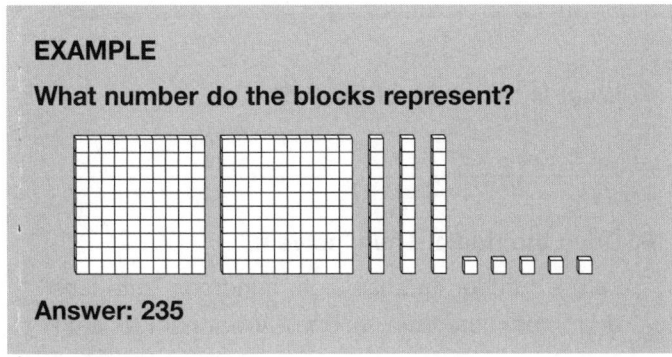

Answer: 235

1. **Which number has seven hundreds, three tens, five ones?**

   (A) 537

   (B) 735

   (C) 705

   (D) 375

Test Tip

Be sure to show all your work and write a complete explanation if the question asks for it.

2. **Sara says she has enough tens to make 100. Is she correct? Write how you know.**

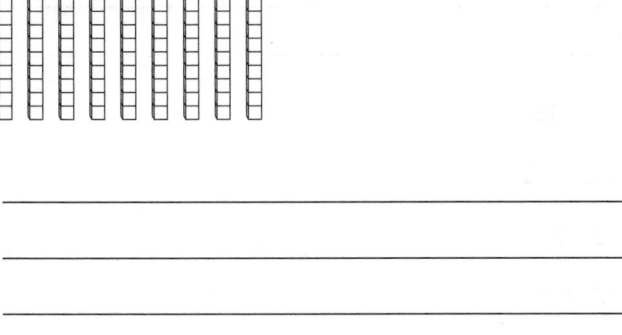

   _____

   _____

   _____

3. **Which picture shows 428?**

   (A)
   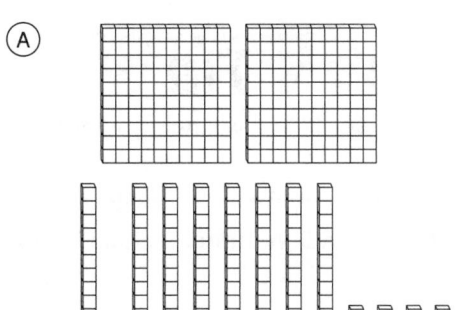

   (B)
   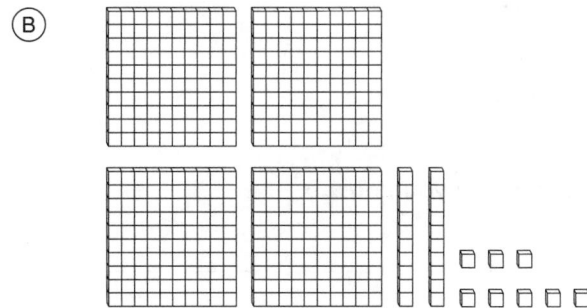

   (C)
   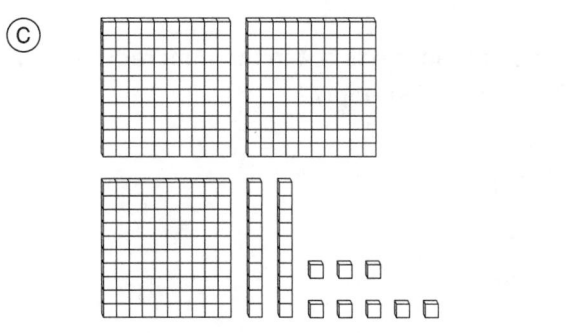

   (D)
   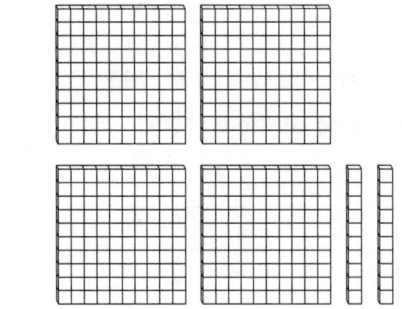

Math

Understand Place Value: Hundreds, Tens, Ones
Number and Operations

Strategy

Use or draw a table to show hundreds, tens, and ones and understand three-digit numbers. For example, for 943, use the table:

Hundreds	Tens	Ones
9	4	3

Test Tip

Underline key words that will help you answer the question.

4. **Which number has a 5 in the tens place? Choose all that apply.**

   (A) 153
   (B) 235
   (C) 859
   (D) 500

   Write how you know.

   _____

   _____

5. **Which number has a 4 in the hundreds place? Choose all that apply.**

   (A) 245
   (B) 461
   (C) 184
   (D) 487

DIRECTIONS: Use the following set of numbers to answer questions 6 and 7.

   791, 792, 793, 794, 795

6. **What is the place of the 7s?**

   _____

7. **What is the place of the 9s?**

   _____

8. **Read the riddle. Then, solve it.**

   I am a number that has eight hundreds, zero tens, and three more than six ones. What number am I?

   _____

9. **Jeremy has 2 hundreds + 0 tens + 0 ones bird stickers. Write the number of bird stickers Jeremy has.**

   _____

DIRECTIONS: For questions 10–14, write the numbers in the correct places in the chart.

Hundreds	Tens	Ones

10. 989

11. 378

12. 209

13. 567

14. 456

Count Within 1,000
Number and Operations

DIRECTIONS: Choose or write the correct answer.

Strategy Use place value to count up and count back using three-digit numbers. For example, for the number 436, use the ones to know that counting up means taking 6 ones and adding one to get 7 ones: 437. You can also use it to count back from 6 ones to 5 ones: 435.

EXAMPLE

What are the next three numbers after 565?

Answer: 566, 567, 568

DIRECTIONS: Write the missing numbers in the blanks for questions 1–3.

1. 432, 433, _____, 435, _____, _____, 438

Write how you know.

_____

_____

_____

2. 898, _____, 900, 901, _____, _____, 904

3. 103, 104, _____, _____, _____, 108

DIRECTIONS: Answer each riddle for questions 4–6.

Test Tip

Look for key words, such as *count back* and *count up*.

4. **What is the next number when you count back from 278?**

_____

Write how you know.

_____

_____

_____

5. **What is the number between 601 and 603?**

_____

6. **What is the number just before 800?**

_____

7. **Write the missing numbers in the chart.**

547		549
690		
	481	

Write how you know.

_____

_____

8. **What numbers go in the blank spaces when you skip count by fives? Choose the best answer.**

65, 70, _____, _____, 85, 90, _____

- Ⓐ 60, 75, 100
- Ⓑ 50, 55, 95
- Ⓒ 75, 80, 95
- Ⓓ 70, 80, 95

Count Within 1,000
Number and Operations

Strategy Use place value to know if you are counting on by hundreds, tens, or ones. So if you are counting on by tens from 33, the answer is 43. If you are counting on by ones from 33, the answer is 34.

9. **How are these two sets of numbers alike?**

45, 55, 65, 75

60, 70, 80, 90

Ⓐ Both count on by 1s.

Ⓑ Both count on by 5s.

Ⓒ Both count on by 10s.

Ⓓ Both count on by 100s.

Write how you know.

_____

_____

_____

_____

10. **How many hundreds make 900?**

_____

Write how you know.

_____

_____

_____

11. **Jon counted the books in the class library. He got to the number 3 hundreds, 1 ten, 6 ones, and counted 5 more books. How many books did Jon count in all? Write how you know.**

_____

_____

_____

12. **Lizzie has read 125 pages of her book. She knows she will read 5 more pages on the bus ride home. How many pages will Lizzie have read after the bus ride? Write how you know.**

_____

_____

_____

13. **Sam counted the pigs on his grandmother's farm. Sam got to 1 hundreds, 1 ten, and 8 ones. He knows that his grandmother gave 5 pigs to her neighbor while he was counting. So he counted back 5 pigs. How many pigs did Sam count? Write how you know.**

_____

_____

_____

Read and Write Numbers to 1,000
Number and Operations

DIRECTIONS: Choose or write the correct answer.

Strategy | Use place value to read, write, and represent numbers using numerals, number names, and expanded form.

EXAMPLE

What is the expanded form and number for seven hundred eighty-six?

Answer: 700 + 80 + 6

786

1. **Which number matches the word?**

> six hundred fifty-six

- (A) 6,506
- (B) 656
- (C) 560
- (D) 5,066

Test Tip

Draw a place-value chart showing hundreds, tens, and ones. Place each digit of the given number in the correct column to help you identify another form of the number.

2. **What word name represents the number?**

> 109

3. **Elsie says that these are the same number. Is Elsie correct? Write how you know.**

> five hundred thirty-two

> 530

4. **Jeff lives at 825 Walnut Street. Which number name means the same as 825?**

- (A) eight hundred fifty-two
- (B) eight hundred thirty-five
- (C) eight hundred twenty-five
- (D) eight hundred eighty-five

5. **Which number is between 375 and 399? Choose all that apply.**

- (A) 300 + 90 + 3
- (B) 300 + 70 + 3
- (C) 300 + 80 + 4
- (D) 300 + 90 + 8

6. **Adam wrote 816 in expanded form. Write what he did wrong.**

> 80 + 10 + 6

Read and Write Numbers to 1,000
Number and Operations

Strategy Write numbers in several ways to make sure you understand their value. The number 678 can be written as: 6 hundreds 7 tens 8 ones; six hundred and seventy-eight; or 600 + 70 + 8.

7. What number do the blocks show?

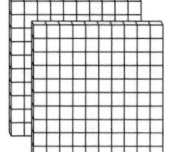 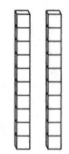

(A) 522

(B) 252

(C) 507

(D) 225

Test Tip

If you are not sure of the answer in a multiple choice question, start by crossing off the answers that could not be right.

8. How many hundreds make 900?

_____

9. Which are the same as 471? Choose all that apply.

(A) 400 + 70 + 1

(B) 400 + 10 + 7

(C) four hundred seventy-one

(D) 4 + 7 + 1

10. Do the word name and the expanded form represent the same number? Write how you know.

| five hundred seventy-four |

| 500 + 40 + 7 |

_____

_____

_____

11. Which is represented by the blocks? Choose all that apply.

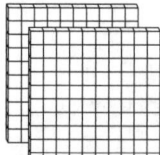 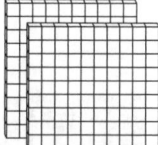 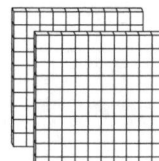

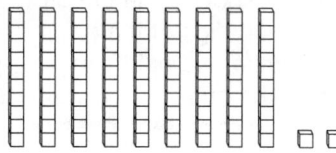

(A) 692

(B) six hundred twenty-nine

(C) six hundred ninety-two

(D) 600 + 20 + 9

Compare Three-Digit Numbers
Number and Operations

DIRECTIONS: Answer the questions.

Strategy

Use place value to compare three-digit numbers. For example, the number 321 is greater than the number 319 because 321 has 3 hundreds, 2 tens, and 1 one. The number 319 has 3 hundreds, 1 ten, and 9 ones. There are more tens in 321.

EXAMPLE

What number makes this sentence true? Choose all that apply.

☐ < 546

(A) 578

(B) 487

(C) 503

(D) 378

Answer: B, C, D

Test Tip

The symbol > means greater than. The open side points toward the larger number. The symbol < means less than. The closed side points to the smaller number. The equal sign, =, means that each side has the same value.

1. Min and Liza each scored 278 points in a game. Which sentence correctly compares their points?

(A) 278 < 278

(B) 278 = 278

(C) 278 > 278

(D) 287 < 278

DIRECTIONS: Write the correct symbol in the box for questions 2–5.

2. 258 ☐ 248

3. 538 ☐ 583

4. 701 ☐ 710

5. 431 ☐ 431

6. Janine writes 427 > 463. She says she is correct because there are 7 ones in 427 and only 3 ones in 463. Is Janine correct? Write how you know.

_____

_____

_____

7. Look at the numbers in the boxes. Write <, >, or = in the ☐ to make each sentence true.

352	361

The number of hundreds in 352 is ☐ the number of hundreds in 361.

The number of tens in 352 is ☐ the number of tens in 361.

The number of ones in 352 is ☐ the number of ones in 361.

8. The Sanchez family wants to buy a new dining table. One table costs $439 and the other $409. Write how to compare the two prices to see which table costs less.

_____

_____

_____

_____

_____

Compare Three-Digit Numbers
Number and Operations

Strategy | To compare three-digit numbers, write them one on top of the other. Then compare how many hundreds, tens, and ones in each.

DIRECTIONS: For questions 9–12, look at the number pairs. Write each number in the pair under the correct label: Greater Number or Lesser Number.

	Greater Number	Lesser Number

9. 145   154

10. 805   895

11. 654   454

12. 913   923

13. Mrs. Raymond read a book that is 564 pages long. Mrs. Simon read a book with an equal number of pages. Which sentence correctly compares the number of pages in the two books?

(A) 568 > 564

(B) 564 < 564

(C) 564 = 564

(D) 563 = 568

14. For the class picnic, Mrs. Haley bought 345 paper plates and 355 paper cups. Write <, >, or = in the ☐. Then, write how you know.

345 ☐ 355

_____

_____

_____

15. Compare the numbers in the chart by writing the number pairs in the correct column. The first one has been done for you.

651 and 435

333 and 444

210 and 189

845 and 846

Greater Number	Lesser Number
651	435

16. 222 is greater than 122. Write how you know.

_____

_____

_____

Test Tip

When you finish your test, go back and make sure you didn't skip any questions.

Add and Subtract Within 100
Number and Operations

DIRECTIONS: Choose or write the correct answer.

Strategy — Use place-value understanding to add and subtract. For two-digit numbers, add or subtract the ones and then, add or subtract the tens.

EXAMPLE

Hayley practiced the piano for 36 minutes on Monday, 25 minutes on Wednesday, and 31 minutes on Friday. How many minutes did she practice in all? Choose the best answer.

(A) 80 minutes

(B) 82 minutes

(C) 97 minutes

(D) 92 minutes

Answer: D

1. A rancher has some horses. He puts 16 horses in each of 3 pens. How many horses does the rancher have? Choose the best answer.

(A) 48

(B) 19

(C) 32

(D) 38

Write how you know.

_____

_____

_____

_____

_____

_____

2. Jerome and his dad are building a fence around their garden. They use 28 long nails and 54 short nails. Write a number sentence to show how many nails they use to build the fence.

_____

DIRECTIONS: Use the table below to answer questions 3 and 4.

Maria's Crayons	
Box of Crayons	Number of Crayons
Box A	8
Box B	16
Box C	32
Box D	42

3. How many crayons does Maria have all together? Write how you know.

_____

_____

4. If Maria gives away Box D to a friend, how many crayons will Maria have left? Write how you know.

_____

_____

_____

5. Add across and down to find the sums. Write the sums in the boxes.

12	30	
46	11	

Add and Subtract Within 100
Number and Operations

Strategy   Write number sentences for word problems to help you understand what is being added or subtracted.

6. **Janie bought some mustard at the store. The mustard cost 67 cents. She bought some yogurt that cost 28 cents more than the mustard. How much did the yogurt cost? Choose the best answer.**

   (A) 39 cents

   (B) 85 cents

   (C) 91 cents

   (D) 95 cents

   Write how you know.

   _____

   _____

   _____

   _____

7. **Jason drew 36 circles on a piece of paper. He colored 15 of them red and 12 of them green. How many circles are other colors? Use words, numbers, or pictures.**

8. **Two girls solved the same problem different ways. Choose one way and explain why it is correct.**

Laura's Way 35 + 25	Lindsay's Way 35 + 25
30 + 20 + 5 +5	25 + 25 + 10

   _____

   _____

   _____

   _____

   DIRECTIONS: Write a number in the ☐ to make the number sentence true for questions 9 and 10.

9. $63 + 14 = \boxed{} + 63$

10. $64 - 10 + 26 = 64 + \boxed{} - 10$

11. **Yuri tried to pick up a box of 51 books. It was too heavy, so he took out 19 books. How many books are now in the box? Solve the problem and show your work. Use words, numbers, or pictures.**

Add and Subtract Within 1,000
Number and Operations

DIRECTIONS: Answer the questions.

Strategy To add and subtract three-digit numbers, use place value: add or subtract the hundreds, then, add or subtract the tens, then, add or subtract the ones.

EXAMPLE

The music store had 457 customers last month and 262 customers this month. How many customers did the store have all together in those two months? Choose the best answer.

Ⓐ 195

Ⓑ 619

Ⓒ 709

Ⓓ 719

Answer: D

Test Tip

You might find it helpful to use scratch paper to draw pictures or record information to solve a problem.

1. Cody played 3 video games. In the first game, he scored 117 points. In the second game, he scored 222 points. In the third game, he scored 60 points less points than in his first game. How many points did he score all together?

Ⓐ 339

Ⓑ 396

Ⓒ 399

Ⓓ 401

Write how you know.

_____

_____

_____

_____

_____

2. Nicole used blocks to solve a problem. Write a number sentence that shows the problem Nicole solved.

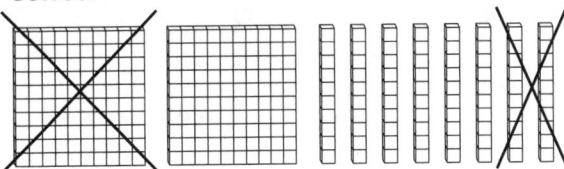

3. One plane has 211 people. Another plane has 328 people. Write in the place-value chart to show how to find the total number of people on the two planes.

	Hundreds	Tens	Ones
Plane 1:			
Plane 2:			
TOTAL:			

Add and Subtract Within 1,000
Number and Operations

Strategy — Draw tables to show hundreds, tens, and ones and compare both three-digit numbers. Or, draw boxes for each place value and compare hundreds, tens, and ones in each number.

Test Tip — Read all parts of the question first.

DIRECTIONS: The chart shows the number of students in Grades 1–4 at Hometown School. Use the chart to answer questions 4–6.

Grade	Number of Students
Grade 1	127
Grade 2	134
Grade 3	111
Grade 4	98

4. How many total students are in grades 1–4?

_____

5. Did you need to regroup to find the total? Write why or why not.

_____

_____

_____

6. How many more students are in grades 1 and 2 than in grades 3 and 4? Write how you know.

_____

_____

_____

7. Lia has 3 packs of sports cards. Pack 1 has 46 cards and pack 2 has 55 cards. Pack 3 has 5 fewer cards than pack 2. Which number sentences can be used to find how many cards Lia has in all? Choose all that apply.

(A) 40 + 50 + 50 + 6 + 5 = 151

(B) 40 + 50 + 6 + 5 = 105

(C) 46 + 55 + 50 = 151

(D) 46 + 55 − 5 = 96

8. For which problems do you need to regroup? Choose all that apply.

(A) 56 + 39

(B) 385 − 142

(C) 912 − 83

(D) 49 + 5

9. The months of September, November, April and June each have 30 days. The blocks below show the number of total days for September, April, and June. Use as few blocks as possible to show the total number of days for September, November, April and June. Draw a picture and write how you know.

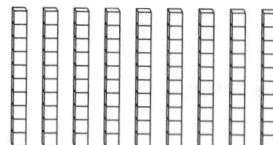

Use Mental Math: Add and Subtract 10 and 100
Number and Operations

DIRECTIONS: Choose or write the correct answer.

Strategy | Use mental math and place value to add and subtract 10 and 100 to greater numbers. Count up or count back by tens or hundreds.

EXAMPLE

There are black and brown beans in a jar. There are 354 brown beans in the jar. There are 100 less black beans than brown beans. How many black beans are in the jar?

Answer: 100 less than 354 is 254.

Test Tip

To quickly add 10 to a number, increase the tens digit by 1. To add 100 to a number, increase the hundreds digit by 1.

DIRECTIONS: Write 10 less and 10 more than the given number for questions 4–7.

1. Cary and Lia are counting their stickers. Cary has 10 more stickers than Lia. Lia has 224 stickers. How many stickers does Cary have?

(A) 214

(B) 324

(C) 124

(D) 234

Write how you know.

_____

_____

4. _____ 653 _____
      10 less   10 more

5. _____ 155 _____
      10 less   10 more

6. _____ 284 _____
      10 less   10 more

7. _____ 711 _____
      10 less   10 more

2. Liza said that 100 more than 562 is 572. What did Liza do wrong?

_____

_____

DIRECTIONS: Write 100 less and 100 more than the given number for questions 8–11.

8. _____ 503 _____
      100 less   100 more

9. _____ 177 _____
      100 less   100 more

3. Mrs. Como read a book with 478 pages. Mr. Como read a book with 100 less pages. How many pages are in Mr. Como's book?

(A) 378

(B) 488

(C) 468

(D) 278

10. _____ 289 _____
      100 less   100 more

11. _____ 891 _____
      100 less   100 more

Use Mental Math: Add and Subtract 10 and 100 to Numbers 100–900

Number and Operations

Strategy

Write a three-digit number in boxes to keep place value in mind. If you are adding or subtracting 657 and 435, write them in boxes to line up place values:

6	5	7
4	3	5

12. Sharon drew a picture with 253 dots on it. She added 100 more dots. What can Sharon do to find how many dots are now in her picture?

- Ⓐ Change 3 to 2
- Ⓑ Change 5 to 4.
- Ⓒ Change 2 to 3.
- Ⓓ Change 2 to 1.

Write how you know.

_____

_____

_____

_____

13. Brad says that to subtract 100 from 450, he can change the 4 to a 5 to make 550. Is Brad correct? Write how you know.

_____

_____

_____

_____

_____

_____

14. Bob counted 678 pennies in his penny jar. His brother added 100 more pennies. What can Bob do to find how many pennies are now in his jar?

- Ⓐ Change 8 to 9
- Ⓑ Change 7 to 8.
- Ⓒ Change 6 to 5.
- Ⓓ Change 6 to 7.

Write how you know.

_____

_____

DIRECTIONS: Use the number cards below for questions 15 and 16.

2	3	4	5	8

15. Make a three-digit number from the number cards and write it in the box. Then, write the number that is 10 less and 10 more on the lines.

_____ ☐ _____
10 less   10 more

16. Make a three-digit number from the number cards and write it in the box. Then, write the number that is 100 less and 100 more on the lines.

_____ ☐ _____
100 less   100 more

Measure Lengths
Measurement and Data

Strategy Measure lengths of objects using the appropriate tools.

DIRECTIONS: Answer the questions.

EXAMPLE

How long is the leaf?

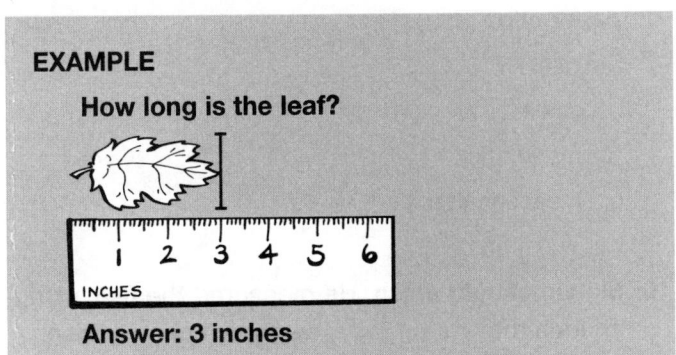

Answer: 3 inches

1. **Which is the BEST tool for Jerome to use to measure how tall he is?**

   (A) ruler

   (B) scale

   (C) thermometer

   (D) meter stick

   Write how you know.

   _____

   _____

   _____

2. **How long is the zipper? Choose the best answer.**

   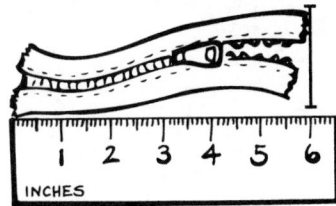

   (A) 1 inch

   (B) 2 inches

   (C) 3 inches

   (D) 6 inches

3. **The ruler below measures inches. Nathan says that the scissors are 4 inches long. Is Nathan correct? Write how you know.**

   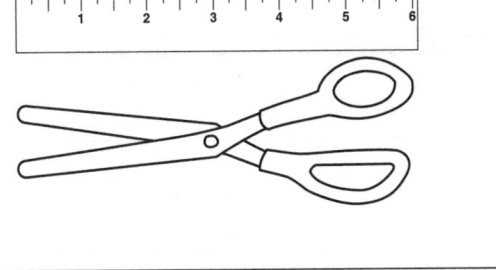

   _____

   _____

   _____

4. **Arlene measured the length of a chain. How many centimeters long is the chain?**

   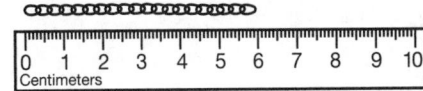

   (A) 6 centimeters

   (B) 5 centimeters

   (C) 7 centimeters

   (D) 8 centimeters

5. **Diane measured the length of a pencil using a centimeter ruler and an inch ruler. Which measure has the greater number of units? Write how you know.**

   _____

   _____

   _____

   _____

Measure Lengths
Measurement and Data

Strategy Read the problem carefully to know exactly what object is being measured.

6. **How many centimeters long are the paper clips? Write how you know.**

```
   0  1  2  3  4  5  6  7  8
   Centimeters
```

_____

_____

_____

_____

7. **Gia is measuring some things in her room. Which things can best be measured with a yardstick? Choose all that apply.**

   (A) bed

   (B) computer screen

   (C) radio

   (D) desk

8. **Sonia measures the length of cloth to make a pair of curtains. The cloth is 82 inches long. Her mother measures the cloth in yards. Sonia says the number of yards will be greater than 82 because yards are larger than inches. Is Sonia correct? Write how you know.**

_____

_____

_____

_____

_____

_____

9. **Which is the best tool to measure, in inches, a large paper clip?**

   (A) ruler

   (B) scale

   (C) meter stick

   (D) measuring tape

10. **Marvin caught a fish. He measured the fish, using an inch measuring tape, as shown below. Then, he measured the same fish and found it measured 22 units long. Which tool did Marvin use that gave him the measure of 22 units?**

_____

_____

_____

_____

_____

_____

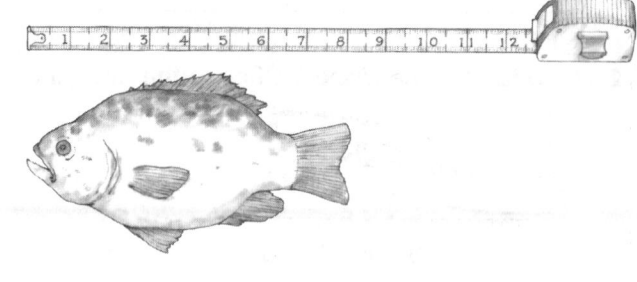

Estimate Lengths
Measurement and Data

DIRECTIONS: Choose or write the correct answer.

Strategy — When exact measurements can't be completed, estimate lengths of objects using inches, feet, and meters.

Test Tip — An estimate is a close guess based on other types of measurements.

EXAMPLE

About how many inches long is a loaf of bread?

Answer: about 12 inches long

1. Estimate the lengths. Choose all that are correct.

(A)

12 yards

(B)

10 meters

(C)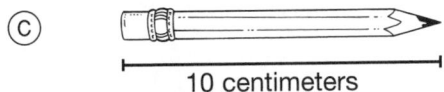

10 centimeters

(D)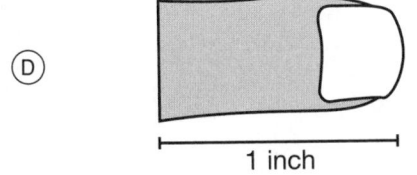

1 inch

2. An apple is next to a paper bag. The bag is about 6 inches tall. About how tall is the apple? Write how you know.

_____

_____

_____

3. About how long is this computer?

(A) 1 inch
(B) 1 foot
(C) 1 yard
(D) 1 meter

Estimate Lengths
Measurement and Data

Strategy | When estimating, compare two objects. Are they about the same size? Is one object half the size of the other object?

4. **Mr. Jackson is about 6 feet tall. He is standing next to his young son. About how tall is his son? Write how you know.**

 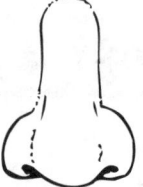

about _____ about _____

_____

_____

_____

5. **Which is closest in length to the watch?**

(A) 5 centimeters

(B) 15 centimeters

(C) 25 centimeters

(D) 35 centimeters

7. **Amy is putting things in a box to take on a family vacation. The box is 4 feet long. What things will fit in the box? Choose all that apply.**

(A) baseball

(B) hammer

(C) desk

(D) skateboard

6. **Estimate the length of each object shown. Choose from the measurements in the box. Write the measurement on the line.**

4 feet 4 meters 2 inches 16 centimeters

about _____ about _____

Find Difference in Lengths
Measurement and Data

DIRECTIONS: Answer the questions.

Strategy   Use adding and subtracting strategies to find the differences in lengths of objects. Find the sum by adding lengths and find the difference by subtracting lengths.

EXAMPLE

Use an inch ruler to measure the arrows. How many inches longer is arrow B than arrow A?

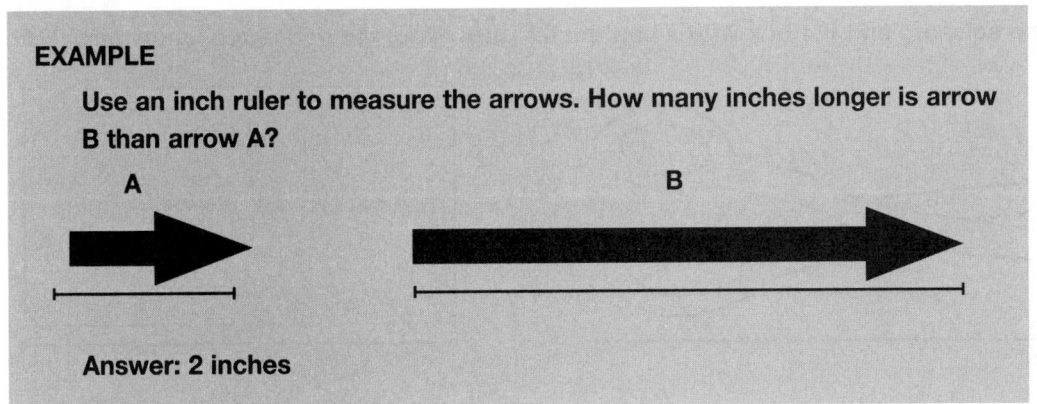

Answer: 2 inches

1. Look at the leaf below. How many inches long must another leaf be to measure 3 inches longer than this leaf?

   (A) 6 inches

   (B) 4 inches

   (C) 3 inches

   (D) 2 inches

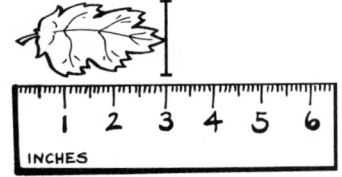

2. Look at the leaf in question 1. What is the difference in length between the leaf and the zipper?

   (A) 3 inches

   (B) 5 inches

   (C) 6 inches

   (D) 9 inches

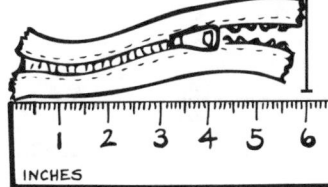

3. Use your centimeter ruler to measure the pencil and the marker. How many centimeters longer is the marker than the pencil? Write how you know.

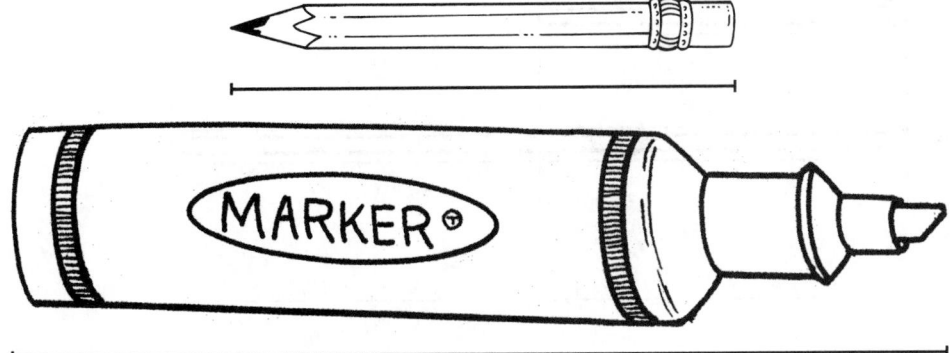

_____

_____

Find Difference in Lengths
Measurement and Data

Strategy Write number sentences to know which measurements to add or subtract and to compare lengths.

DIRECTIONS: Use the pictures of the scissors and box to answer questions 4 and 5.

4. Measure the scissors and the box with a centimeter ruler. Write the measures below each item.

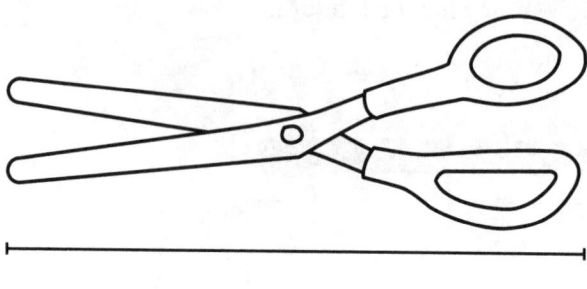
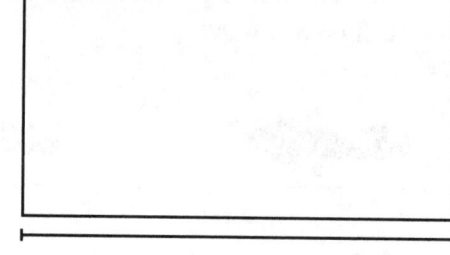

_____ centimeters

_____ centimeters

5. Do the scissors fit in the box? Write how you know.

_____

_____

_____

6. Jason measured the two straws. He says that straw A is 1 inch shorter than straw B. Is Jason correct? Write how you know.

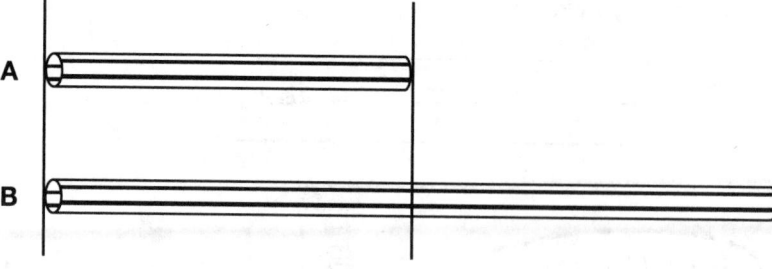

_____

_____

_____

Solve Length Problems: Add and Subtract
Measurement and Data

DIRECTIONS: Answer the questions.

Strategy | Read word problems carefully to identify clue words about adding or subtracting to solve problems about length.

EXAMPLE

Mr. Snell has two pieces of wood. The total length of the two pieces of wood is 35 feet. One piece is 18 feet long. Which is a way to find the length of the second piece of wood? Choose all that apply.

(A) 18 + ☐ = 35

(B) 35 + ☐ = 18

(C) 35 + 18 = ☐

(D) 35 − 18 = ☐

Answer: A, D

Test Tip | Draw a picture to help you answer the problem.

1. At the basketball game, Lee made a basket from 33 feet away. Last year he made a basket from 24 feet away. Write a number sentence to find how much farther away Lee made a basket last year than this year. Then, solve the problem. Use a ? for the unknown number.

_____

_____

2. Haley made a scarf that is 48 inches long. Luz made a scarf that is 5 inches shorter than Haley's. What is the total length of both scarves? Show how you found the answer.

_____

3. Leon measured these two leaves. Then, he found another leaf and measured it. The third leaf is 10 inches long. What is the total length of the 3 leaves?

(A) 3 inches

(B) 6 inches

(C) 13 inches

(D) 16 inches

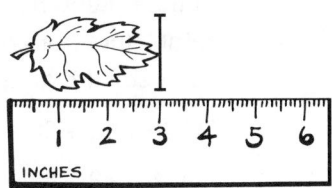 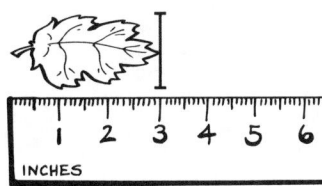

Determine Difference in Lengths
Measurement and Data

Strategy   Use number sentences to solve problems about length.

1. How much longer is the long straw than the short straw?

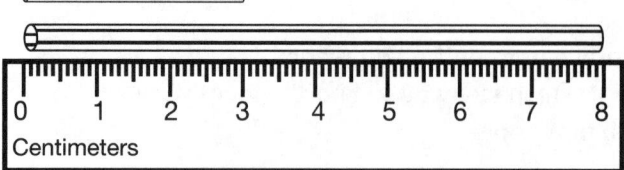

- (A) 9 centimeters
- (B) 6 centimeters
- (C) 5 centimeters
- (D) 3 centimeters

2. Mr. Kim is putting a fence around his garden. He will put these two pieces of fence together to make one side. What is the total length of the two pieces of fence? Write a number sentence to find the total length. Use a ? for the unknown number. Then, solve the problem.

48 inches   48 inches

_____

3. Is the longest pencil longer or shorter than the total length of the other three pencils? Write how you know.

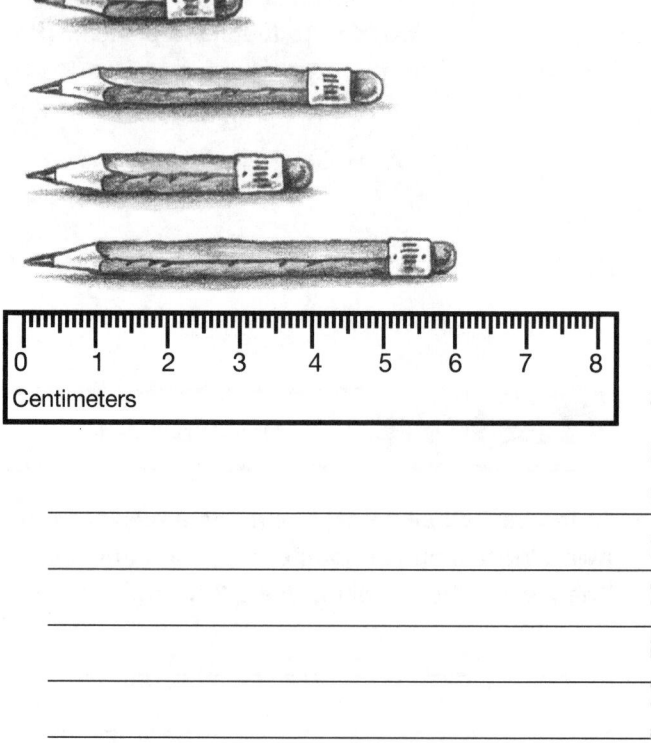

_____
_____
_____
_____
_____
_____

4. Rachel rode her bike to get ready for a race. Rachel rode 26 kilometers on Monday and 48 kilometers on Wednesday. On Friday, Rachel rode 12 fewer kilometers than on Wednesday. Which number sentence can be used to find how many total kilometers Rachel rode on the three days? Choose all that apply.

- (A) $48 + 12 + 26 + 48 = \square$
- (B) $26 + 48 + 48 - 12 = \square$
- (C) $26 + 48 - 12 + 48 = \square$
- (D) $48 + 48 + 12 + 26 = \square$

Telling Time
Measurement and Data

Strategy   Use analog and digital clocks to solve problems about time.

Test Tip   Remember that some clocks use the short hand to show the hour and the long hand to show the minutes.

EXAMPLE

How are the clocks alike? Choose all that apply.

Clock A   Clock B

(A) They show the same time.

(B) They show the hour and the minutes.

(C) They have an hour hand and a minute hand.

(D) The time shown on Clock A is 5 minutes more than the time shown on Clock B.

(E) The time shown is 6:15.

Answer: The two clocks show the same time, 5:15. So, A and B are correct. Only Clock B has an hour hand and a minute hand so C is not correct. And because the time shown, 5:15, is the same for both clocks, D and E are not correct.

1. Which clocks show 10:30? Choose all that apply

(A)    (B)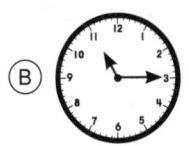

(C)    (D)

2. Clock A below shows the time Kim and Soo Lee went to the park. They were at the park for 30 minutes. Kim says that Clock B shows the time she and Soo Lee left the park. Is Kim correct? Tell why or why not. Use words, numbers, or pictures.

Clock A   Clock B

3. Jason bushed his teeth before going to school in the morning. What could be the time Jason brushed his teeth? Write a time. Use A.M. or P.M. after the time. Then, tell how you know it is A.M. or P.M.

_____

_____

4. Lydia says she can walk to school in 15 minutes. Her brother Kyle says he can walk to school in 5 minutes less time. The clock below shows the time Lydia and Kyle leave for school. Write the time Kyle gets to school. Tell how you know. Use words, pictures or numbers.

Solve Problems: Money
Measurement and Data

DIRECTIONS: Answer the questions.

Strategy Use counting, adding, and subtracting to solve money word problems involving dollar bills, quarters, dimes, nickels, and pennies.

EXAMPLE

Notebooks at the school store cost 60¢ each. Pens cost 35¢ each. Hal has the coins below. Does he have enough money to buy one pen and one notebook? Write how you know.

Answer: No. Hal needs 95¢ and the coins show on 85¢.

1. Michael has 4 quarters and 2 dimes for bus fare. If the bus ride costs 75¢, how much money will he have left?

  Ⓐ 75¢

  Ⓑ 45¢

  Ⓒ 20¢

  Ⓓ 70¢

2. Arnie wants to buy 3 books. Each book costs $1.00. Arnie has the money shown below. Does he have enough money to buy the books? Write how you know. How much will it cost to pay for all the books?

_____

_____

_____

3. Rayna wants to buy a toy that costs one dollar. She has the coins below. How much more money does she need? Choose all that apply.

  Ⓐ

  Ⓑ

  Ⓒ

  Ⓓ

4. Melinda has the money shown below. Draw coins to show the same amount 2 more ways.

Name _____ Date _____

Math

Represent and Interpret Data: Line Plots
Measurement and Data

DIRECTIONS: Choose or write the correct answer.

Strategy | Use line plots by representing measurements to answer questions.

1. Luann measured some lengths of ribbon. The line plot shows the measurements. What is true about the measurements?

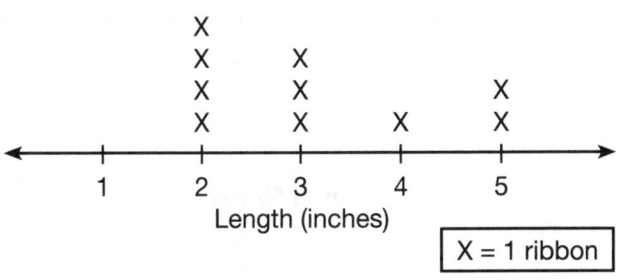

Luann's Ribbons

Length (inches)

X = 1 ribbon

(A) There are more ribbons longer than 3 inches than shorter than 3 inches.

(B) The longest ribbons are 2 inches long.

(C) There are no ribbons longer than 1 inch.

(D) There is 1 ribbon that is 4 inches long.

2. Kevin measured the lengths of the paper chains he made. He recorded the results in a line plot. How many of the paper chains are 4 feet long?

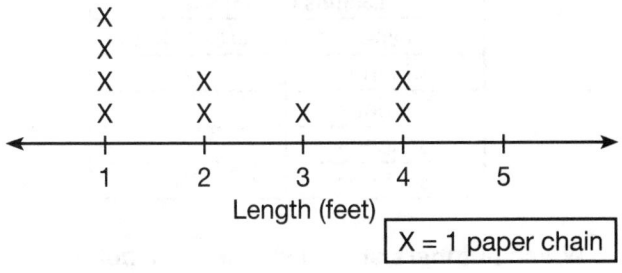

Kevin's Paper Chains

Length (feet)

X = 1 paper chain

_____

DIRECTIONS: Jonas measures some boards he will use to build a dog house. The lengths are shown in the line plot below. Use the line plot to answer questions 3–5.

Board Lengths

Length (feet)

X = 1 board

3. **How many boards does Jonas have?**

(A) 15

(B) 8

(C) 50

(D) 20

4. **Jonas says that the line plot shows that there is only one board more than 11 feet long. Write two more statements that are true about the line plot.**

_____

_____

_____

5. **Jonas needs 5 boards that are greater than 10 feet long. Does he have what he needs? Write how you know.**

_____

_____

_____

Represent and Interpret Data: Line Plots
Measurement and Data

Strategy Remember that line plots show problems visually. Use or draw other pictures to help you answer questions.

6. Marcus is cutting straws into different lengths to use for an art project. The lengths are shown in the table below. Which line plot correctly shows the data in Marcus' table?

Lengths of Straws	
10 inches	3
8 inches	6
6 inches	4
4 inches	5

Ⓐ **Lengths of Straws**

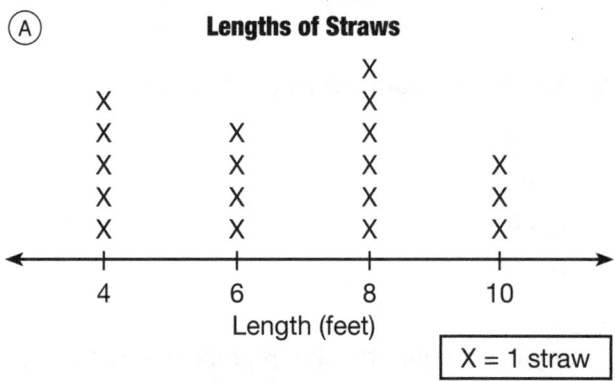

Ⓑ **Lengths of Straws**

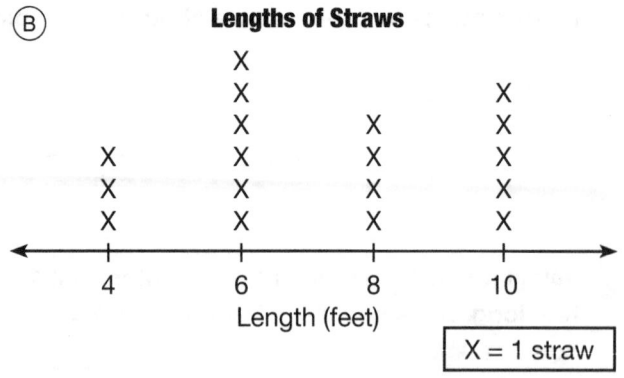

Ⓒ **Lengths of Straws**

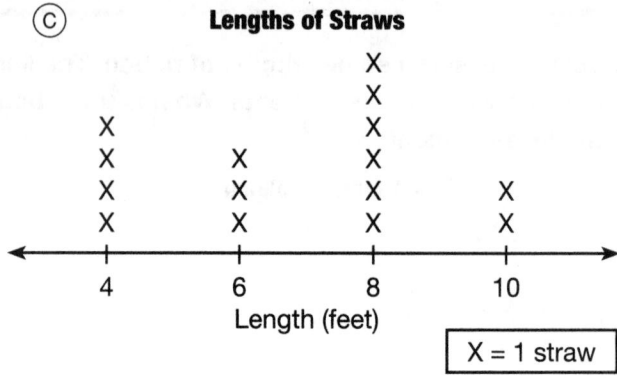

Ⓓ **Lengths of Straws**

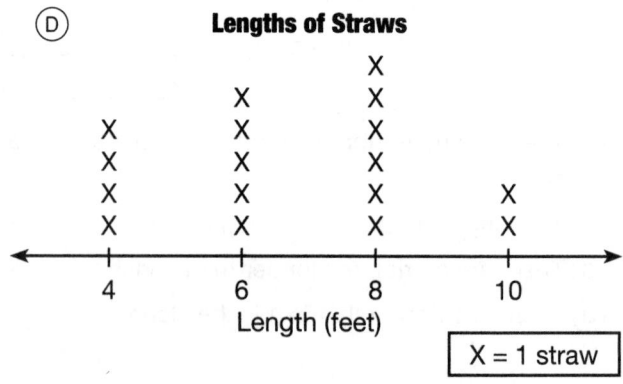

DIRECTIONS: Luisa cut some string to use for wrapping packages. She made this table of her measurements and wants to make a line plot of the data.

Lengths of Markers	
Inches	**Pieces of String**
4 inches	2
5 inches	4
6 inches	7
8 inches	10

7. Which numbers should she use to label the lengths on the line plot? Choose all that apply.

Ⓐ 2

Ⓑ 5

Ⓒ 10

Ⓓ 4

Draw and Interpret Graphs
Measurement and Data

Strategy Represent data on picture graphs and bar graphs in order to interpret, or explain, it.

DIRECTIONS: The second-grade students in Mrs. Paul's and Miss Fanta's classes voted on where they would go on a field trip. Their votes are shown in the pictograph below. Use the pictograph to answer the questions.

Test Tip

When reading a pictograph, use the key to tell you what each picture stands for.

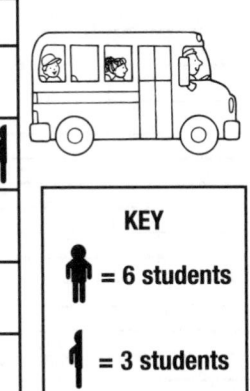

Votes for Class Trip	
Place	**Votes**
Animal Park	🚶🚶🚶🚶
Museum	🚶🚶
Theater	🚶🚶
Nature Center	🚶🚶🚶

KEY
🚶 = 6 students
🚶 = 3 students

1. How many students voted to go to the theater?

Ⓐ 15
Ⓑ 11
Ⓒ 9
Ⓓ 6

2. Which place received more votes than the museum? Choose all that apply.

Ⓐ animal park
Ⓑ museum
Ⓒ theater
Ⓓ nature center

3. Which place received the most votes?

_____

4. Which place received the least numbers of votes?

_____

5. What is the total number of students who voted? Show how you got your answer.

_____

_____

_____

6. How many more students voted for the nature center than the museum? Show how you got your answer.

_____

_____

7. Jamal said that if 6 more students chose to go to the nature center, the nature center would have the most votes. Is Jamal correct? Write why or why not.

_____

_____

_____

_____

_____

Draw and Interpret Graphs
Measurement and Data

Strategy Read all parts of a table, graph, or picture to identify the information presented.

DIRECTIONS: Tia was helping out in her dad's shoe store. She thinks that the store sells more of some sizes than others. Tia kept track of how many shoes were sold in each size for three days. Her results are shown in the table below. Use the table to help you complete the bar graph.

Test Tip A bar graph shows you more or fewer by how tall each bar is. The lower the bar, the lesser amount it stands for.

Shoe Size	Total Pairs Sold
5	3
6	10
7	8
8	6

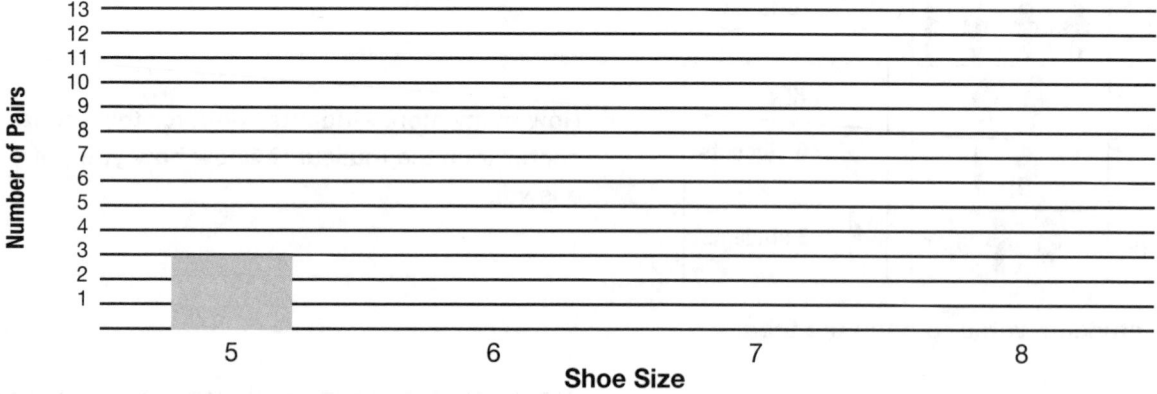

8. **Add the bars missing from the graph to show the number of shoes sold in each size.**

9. **What does Tia know from all of the information she has gathered? Choose all that apply.**

   Ⓐ More size 5 that size 8 shoes were sold.

   Ⓑ More size 7 shoes than size 8 shoes were sold.

   Ⓒ More size 6 shoes than size 7 shoes were sold.

   Ⓓ More size 8 shoes than size 7 shoes were sold.

10. **Was Tia correct in thinking the store sells more of some sizes than others? Write how you know, using information from the graph.**

   _____

   _____

   _____

Name _____ Date _____

Math

Recognize and Draw Shapes
Geometry

DIRECTIONS: Choose or write the correct answer.

Strategy   Identify and draw shapes based on how many angles and sides they have.

EXAMPLE

What is the name of this shape? How do you know?

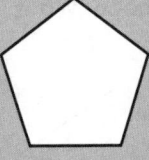

Answer: pentagon; a pentagon has 5 sides and 5 angles.

Test Tip

Count the number of sides and angles a shape has to help determine its name.

1. **Which shape has one less angle than a square? Choose all that apply.**

 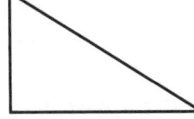

2. **Which shape has no sides or angles?**

 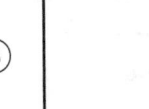

3. **What is the name of a shape that has one more side than a square?**

_____

Recognize and Draw Shapes
Geometry

Strategy Make a table of each shape, drawing the shape, writing its name, and then writing the number of sides.

DIRECTIONS: Use the shapes inside the box to answer questions 4 and 5.

4. How many of these shapes have four or more sides?

_____

5. Name the shapes that do not have 4 or more sides.

_____

DIRECTIONS: Use the picture below to answer questions 6 and 7.

6. What is the name of this shape?

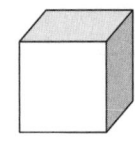

_____

7. What shape is the face of the cube?

_____

DIRECTIONS: Use the shape below to answer questions 8 and 9.

8. Janine drew this shape. What is the name of the shape?

- Ⓐ quadrilateral
- Ⓑ pentagon
- Ⓒ hexagon
- Ⓓ triangle

9. How do knowing the attributes of the shape help you name it?

_____

_____

_____

_____

10. Draw a closed shape that has fewer angles than a pentagon. Tell the name of the shape you drew.

Partition Rectangles
Geometry

DIRECTIONS: Choose or write the correct answer.

Strategy   Use shapes and equal parts to divide rectangles into same-size squares and determine the total number of squares.

EXAMPLE

Daro divided the shape below into equal parts. How many equal parts are in the shape?

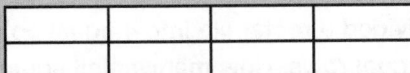

Answer: 8 equal parts

Test Tip

Pay attention to the numbers in the problem and the answer choices. If you misread even one number, you may choose the wrong answer.

3. Liam counted 12 small squares in a rectangle. Make a drawing of the rectangle Liam might have seen. Use a ruler to draw your lines.

1. Ava divided a rectangle into 6 equal parts. Which of these shows Ava's rectangle?

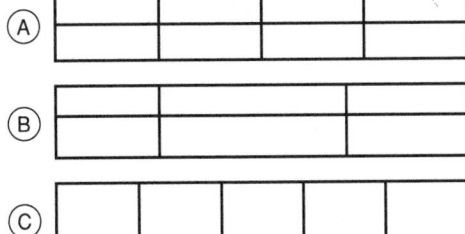

4. Milo drew these two shapes. How many parts are in each shape?

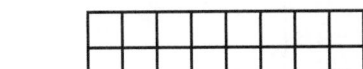

2. Sophia is covering the shape below with gray tiles. The gray tiles are all the same size and shape. How many more gray tiles does Sophia need to cover the shape?

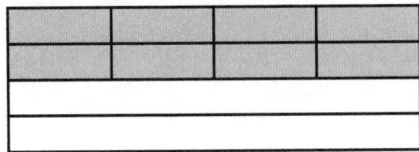

(A) 20

(B) 8

(C) 5

(D) 4

Partition Rectangles
Geometry

Strategy — Compare shapes to find similarities, such as the number of sides. Use your comparisons to understand how shapes fit within other shapes.

5. Draw lines on the rectangle below to show the same number of equal parts. Use a ruler to draw your lines.

_____

Test Tip

Before you choose or write an answer, ask yourself: "Does this answer make sense?"

7. Luca divided a rectangle into 4 equal columns and 6 equal rows. How many small squares are in his rectangle?

_____

6. Mia wants to cover her paper below with squares all the same size. She has placed 2 squares on the paper and has 6 squares left. Does Mia have enough squares left to cover her paper picture? Write how you know.

_____

_____

_____

_____

_____

_____

Name _____ Date _____

Math

Partition Circles and Rectangles Equally
Geometry

DIRECTIONS: Choose or write the correct answer.

Strategy — Use the attributes of circles and rectangles to divide them into equal shares and describe the shares using halves, thirds, and fourths.

EXAMPLE

How many equal shares are in this rectangle?

What are the shares called?

How many shares make up the whole?

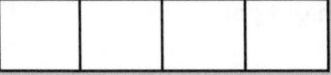

Answer: 4 equal shares. The shares are called fourths. The whole is four fourths.

1. How many parts does this circle have?

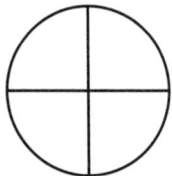

(A) 1
(B) 3
(C) 4
(D) 5

2. How many parts of the rectangle are shaded?

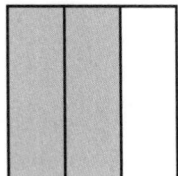

(A) one half
(B) one third
(C) two fourths
(D) two thirds

3. Dani says that the shape below has two halves. Is Dani correct? Write how you know.

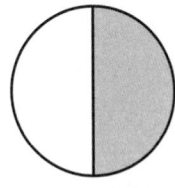

_____

_____

_____

_____

4. How many parts of this circle are shaded?

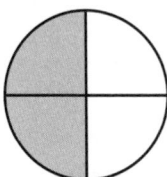

(A) one half
(B) one third
(C) two thirds
(D) one quarter

Partition Circles and Rectangles into Equal Shares

Geometry

Strategy   Count each part to identify the whole. Then, determine if all the parts are equal.

Test Tip   Remember that sharing equally means that each person gets the same amount or size.

5. Jeremy and Darren each ate a whole pizza as shown below. Rocco said he ate more pizza because he ate 4 pieces. Is Rocco correct? Tell why or why not.

Jeremy's Pizza   Darren's Pizza   Rocco's Pizza

_____

_____

_____

_____

_____

6. Tim, Tom, and Tina split a pie. They ate it all. Each got the same size piece. Which picture shows how they cut the pie? Choose all that apply.

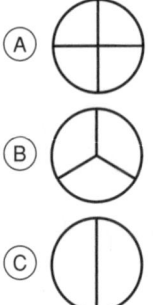

7. Catie and Nina split a pizza. Each got the same size piece. Draw on the pizza below to show how they cut the pizza. Then, tell what part of the pizza each girl got.

8. Four friends shared a pie. Each got the same size piece. Which picture shows how they cut the pie?

Strategy Review

In this section, you will review the strategies you learned and apply them to practice the skills.

Strategy — Use basic operations to solve word problems.

EXAMPLE

Thad has 16 baseball cards and 40 football cards. He buys some soccer cards and now has 67 sports cards. Write a number sentence that you can use to find how many soccer cards Thad bought. Use a ☐ for the number of soccer cards. Then, solve it.

First, write a number sentence.

$67 - 16 - 40 = ☐$.

Then, solve your number sentence.

$67 = 16 = 51; 51 - 40 = 11$

EXAMPLE

Freda told her teacher how she added $43 + 55$.

First, she broke the numbers into tens and ones.

$40 + 50 + 3 + 5$.

Next, she added the tens, and the ones.

$40 + 50 = 90; 3 + 5 = 8$

She combined the tens and ones.

$90 + 8 = 98$

So, $43 + 55 = 98$

1. A farmer has 75 ears of corn. He sells 14 ears at his stand. Then, he picks 11 more ears of corn. How many ears of corn does the farmer have now?

   Ⓐ 24
   Ⓑ 72
   Ⓒ 89
   Ⓓ 100

2. There were 67 tickets left to sell for the school fair. In the morning, some of the tickets were sold. There are 32 tickets still left to sell. How many tickets were sold in the morning?

   Ⓐ 35
   Ⓑ 32
   Ⓒ 53
   Ⓓ 99

3. Jayne and Nona look for bird nests in the field for 4 months. The table below shows how many nests they found each month.

Month	Number of Nests
1	25
2	13
3	18
4	32

4. Choose all the ways to find the total number of nests Jayne and Nona found in four months.

   Ⓐ $25 + 13 + 18 + 32$
   Ⓑ $30 + 10 + 10 + 20 + 2 + 8 + 3 + 5$
   Ⓒ $13 + 32 + 25 + 18$
   Ⓓ $20 + 10 + 5 + 1$

Strategy Review

Strategy Use what you know about numbers to answer questions.

EXAMPLE

Hundreds	Tens	Ones
4	3	8

Use place value to know that the number can be read as four hundred thirty-eight, and written as 400 + 30 + 8.

1. What is another way to write 651? Choose all that apply.

   Ⓐ 6 hundred fifty-one

   Ⓑ 60 + 5 + 1

   Ⓒ 600 + 50 + 1

   Ⓓ 6 hundreds 5 tens 1 one

2. Lydia's game score has 3 digits. The digit 7 is in the tens place. The other digits are 1 and 6. What could be Lydia's score? Show how you know.

   _____

   _____

   _____

   _____

3. What three numbers are missing?

   556, _____, _____, 559, _____, 561

4. Jerrod has 362 pennies. Jorge has 289 pennies. Use <, =, or > to write a number sentence that compares the number of pennies Jerrod has to the number of pennies Jorge has.

   _____

Strategy Choose the right tool and units to measure objects.

EXAMPLE

Use a ruler to measure the length of a spoon or book. Use a meter stick or yardstick to measure the length of a desk. Use a measuring tape to measure how tall you are.

5. Which of these is best measured with a ruler? Choose all that apply.

   Ⓐ

   Ⓑ

   Ⓒ

   Ⓓ

Strategy Review

1. How long is the zipper?

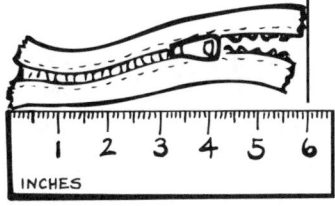

_____

2. Which is about 2 meters in length?

(A) bus

(B) bicycle

(C) pencil

(D) scissors

3. Val's snake is 25 centimeters long. Trina's snake is 13 centimeters longer than Val's snake. Show how to find how long Val's snake is. Use words, numbers, or pictures.

First, think about what you are being asked to find.

You need to read the clock and add a half hour to find what time he eats lunch.

Half an hour after 11:30 is 12:00. He eats lunch at 12:00.

4. The clock shows the time Felix plays soccer on Saturday morning. Felix plays for 25 minutes. What time does Felix finish playing soccer?

(A) 11:25 a.m.

(B) 11:40 a.m.

(C) 11:40 p.m.

(D) 11:25 p.m.

5. Marcus has the money shown below. How many dollars and cents does he have? Use the symbols $ and ¢ in your answer.

_____

Strategy

Read word problems carefully. Make sure you know what you are asked to do.

EXAMPLE

Use a clock to tell time. The clock shows the time. Ernie eats lunch in half an hour. What time does he eat lunch?

Math

Strategy Review

DIRECTIONS: Use the picture graph below to answer the questions.

Strategy

Use graphs and drawings to understand numbers.

EXAMPLE

A picture graph uses symbols or pictures in place of a number. The key tells what number each picture stands for. How many students does each 𝗑 stand for in the key below?

Key: 𝗑 5 students   Answer: 5 students

Grade Level	Number of Students
Kindergarten	𝗑𝗑𝗑𝗑𝗑𝗑𝗑𝗑𝗑
1st Grade	𝗑𝗑𝗑𝗑𝗑𝗑𝗑𝗑𝗑𝗑𝗑𝗑𝗑
2nd Grade	𝗑𝗑𝗑𝗑𝗑𝗑
3rd Grade	𝗑𝗑𝗑𝗑𝗑𝗑𝗑𝗑
4th Grade	𝗑𝗑𝗑𝗑𝗑𝗑𝗑𝗑𝗑𝗑𝗑𝗑
5th Grade	𝗑𝗑𝗑𝗑𝗑𝗑𝗑

Key: 𝗑 = 5 students

1. What grade level has the fewest students? Write how you know.

_____

_____

2. How many more students are in 1st grade than in 3rd grade? Show your work.

_____

_____

Strategy

Use what you know about numbers, shapes, and measurement to answer questions.

EXAMPLE

Name the shape that has these attributes:

- 4 equal sides
- 4 equal angles

The shape is a square.

DIRECTIONS: Gia and Malani each cut out some shapes to make a picture. One of the shapes is shown below. Use the shapes to answer questions 1 and 2.

Gia's

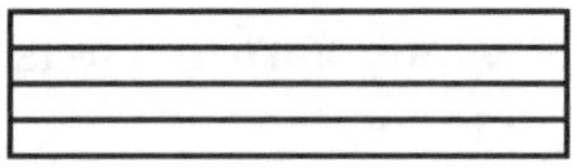

Malani's

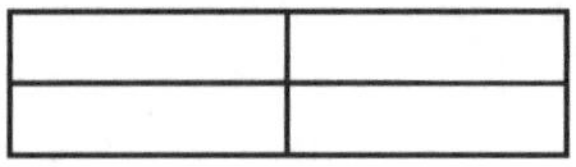

3. What is the name of the shape the girls cut out? Write how you know.

_____

_____

4. Malani thinks her pieces are larger than Gia's. Is she correct? Why or why not?

_____

_____

_____

_____

_____

_____

Describe a Story
Reading: Literature

DIRECTIONS: Read the story. Then, answer the questions keeping the characters, setting, and what happens in mind.

Invisible Cassie

Cassie kicked at the dirty clothes on her floor. She was upset. Her dad told her to clean her room. Cassie wished she were invisible. Then, she wouldn't have to clean anything! If she were invisible, she would go to school and not do any work. She would stay up late. She would never have to take baths. Best of all, her brother couldn't pick on her. But, wait! If she were invisible, she wouldn't get any apple pie. No one would ask her to play. Cassie would never get to hug her grandparents. Maybe being invisible wouldn't be so much fun after all.

Strategy — Identify and make a list of the parts of a story: characters, setting, and what happens.

Test Tip — A story usually tells what characters think or how they feel.

1. What is Cassie's problem in the beginning of the story?
   - Ⓐ She wants to visit her grandparents.
   - Ⓑ She can't have any apple pie.
   - Ⓒ She has a brother who teases her.
   - ● She doesn't want to clean her room.

What details in the story tell you about Cassie's problem? Choose all that apply.
   - ● "Cassie kicked at the dirty clothes on her floor."
   - ● "She was upset."
   - ● "Her dad told her to clean her room"
   - Ⓓ "Best of all, her brother couldn't pick on her."

2. **Write two details that tell why Cassie thinks being invisible is a good solution to her problem.**
   Possible Answers: She would go to school and not do any work. She would stay up late. She would never have to take baths. Her brother couldn't pick on her.

3. Who is the main character in the story?
   - Ⓐ Cassie's dad
   - ● Cassie
   - Ⓒ Cassie's grandparents
   - Ⓓ Cassie's brother

Write how you know.
   Possible Answer: All of the key details are about Cassie and her thoughts and feelings about being invisible.

4. Which sentences from the story tell why Cassie wouldn't want to be invisible? Choose all that apply.
   - Ⓐ "Best of all, her brother couldn't pick on her."
   - ● "If she were invisible she wouldn't get any apple pie."
   - ● "Cassie would never get to hug her grandparents."
   - Ⓓ "She would stay up late."

7

Describe a Story
Reading: Literature

DIRECTIONS: Read the story. Then, answer the questions using details from the story and the picture.

The Oldest

Sometimes, Sam likes being the oldest. He can stay up one hour later. He can go places by himself. He also gets a bigger allowance for helping around the house. When his friend Brennan asks him to spend the night, Sam's mom says yes. He even gets to stay at his friend's house to eat dinner sometimes. Sam thinks it's great that he can read, ride a bike, and spell better than his brother. Sam's sister loves when he reads stories to her. Sam likes it, too. When his mom needs help cooking, she asks Sam, because he is the oldest.

Sometimes, Sam doesn't like being the oldest. He has to babysit his sister. She likes to go where he does. He also has to act more like a grown-up. Sam always has more jobs to do around the house. He has to help wash the dishes and take out the trash. His brother and sister get help when they have to clean their rooms. Sam doesn't get help. Sam doesn't like to be the oldest when his brother and sister want him to play with them all the time.

Strategy — Ask yourself Who, What, and Where questions to figure out the parts of a story.

Test Tip — Look for who the story is mostly about to find the main character.

1. Who is the main character in the story?
   - ● Sam
   - Ⓑ Mom
   - Ⓒ Brennan
   - Ⓓ Sam's sister

Write how you know.
   Possible Answer: The story tells what Sam thinks and how he feels.

2. Which detail tells how Sam thinks or feels?
   - Ⓐ He likes to help his mother with the cooking.
   - Ⓑ He thinks his sister should read more stories.
   - ● He doesn't like it when he has to act like a grown-up.
   - Ⓓ He wants his parents to treat his brother like they treat him.

3. Write a detail from the story that tells how Sam's parents treat him like a grown-up.
   Possible Answers: He has to babysit his sister. Sam always has more jobs to do around the house. He has to help wash the dishes and take out the trash. Sam doesn't get help cleaning his room.

4. What is this story mostly about?
   Possible Answer: The reasons Sam likes and doesn't like being the oldest.

5. The story is organized into two parts or ideas. The first part tells about why Sam likes being the oldest. The second part tells about why Sam _____,
   - Ⓐ likes to have dinner at Brennan's house
   - Ⓑ helps his brother and sister clean their rooms
   - Ⓒ wants to play all the time
   - ● doesn't like being the oldest

8

Recount Stories
Reading: Literature

DIRECTIONS: Read the story. Then, answer the questions using key details from the story.

Strategy — While reading, identify the lesson learned from the story. This is the moral of the story.

Adapted from "The Frog Who Wished to Be as Big as an Ox" by Aesop

One day, an ox was grazing in a meadow. Suddenly, he stepped on a young frog and crushed him to death. The frog's brothers and sisters ran to tell their mother what had happened.

"The monster that did it was such a size, Mother!" they said.

The mother was a vain old thing. She thought that she could easily make herself as large.

"Was it as big as this?" she asked, blowing and puffing herself out.

"Oh, much bigger than that," replied the young frogs.

"As this, then?" she cried, puffing and blowing again with all her might.

"No, mother," they said, "if you were to try till you burst yourself, you could never be so big."

That silly old frog! She tried to puff herself out still more, and burst herself indeed.

1. These events from the story are out of order. Write the numbers 2, 3, 4, 5, 6, and 7 to retell the story in the correct order.
   - ☐1☐ An ox was grazing in a meadow.
   - ☐3☐ The frog's brothers and sisters ran home to tell their mother.
   - ☐5☐ The mother frog puffed and blew, and tried to make herself as big as an ox.
   - ☐2☐ The ox stepped on a frog and crushed it.
   - ☐4☐ The mother thought she could be as big as an ox.
   - ☐6☐ The frogs told their mother she could never be as big as the ox.
   - ☐7☐ The mother tried to puff herself out still more.
   - ☐8☐ The mother frog burst.

2. What do you think the moral of this story is?
   - Ⓐ Don't puff yourself up or you will burst.
   - Ⓑ Don't step on frogs.
   - Ⓒ Don't tell your mother when an ox crushes your brother.
   - ● Don't try to be something you're not.

Write why you think that is the lesson.
   Possible Answer: Frogs are not meant to be as big as an ox, but the mother frog was trying to make herself that big. She lost who she was in the process.

4. Chose two adjectives that describe the mother frog.
   - ● silly
   - Ⓑ brave
   - ● proud
   - Ⓓ smart

5. What do you think the word vain means in the sentence, "The mother was a vain old thing."
   Possible Answer: I think it means a person who wants to always be better than someone else.

9

Recount Stories
Reading: Literature

DIRECTIONS: Read the story. Then, answer the questions.

Strategy — After reading the questions, reread the story and find the answers.

Adapted from "THE COFFEE-MAKING"
(an American Indian story)

One summer afternoon my mother left me alone in our wigwam while she went across the way to my aunt's home. A short while later, a hand lifted the canvas covering of the entrance. It was an old grandfather who had often told me legends of our people.

"Where is your mother, my little grandchild?" were his first words.

"My mother is soon coming back from my aunt's tepee," I replied.

"I shall wait for her return," he said, sitting on a mat.

At once I began to play the part of a kind hostess. I turned to my mother's coffeepot. Lifting the lid, I found nothing but coffee grounds in the bottom. I set the pot on a heap of cold ashes and filled it half full of warm Missouri River water. Then, I placed a small piece of bread in a bowl. I poured out a cup of worse than muddy warm water. I handed the light luncheon to the old warrior.

I was proud to have succeeded so well in serving refreshments to a guest all by myself. Before the old warrior had finished eating, my mother entered. She wondered where I had found coffee. She knew I had never made any before. She also knew that she had left the coffeepot empty. Answering the question in my mother's eyes, the warrior remarked, "My granddaughter made coffee on a heap of dead ashes, and served me the moment I came."

They both laughed, and mother said, "Wait a little longer, and I shall build a fire." They treated my best judgment, poor as it was, with the utmost respect.

6. These events from the story are out of order. Write the numbers 2, 3, 4, 5, 6, and 7 to retell the story in the correct order.
   - ☐1☐ The girl's mother left her alone in the wigwam.
   - ☐3☐ The girl saw that there were only old coffee grounds in the coffee pot.
   - ☐5☐ The girl placed a small piece of bread in a bowl.
   - ☐7☐ The girl's mother came home and offered to make a fire.
   - ☐2☐ An old grandfather came to the wigwam.
   - ☐4☐ The girl poured warm river water into the coffee pot.
   - ☐6☐ The girl served the coffee and bread to the grandfather.
   - ☐8☐ The girl's mother and the warrior treated her best judgment with respect.

7. Choose two adjectives that describe the grandfather.
   - Ⓐ brave
   - ● kind
   - ● respectful
   - Ⓓ mean

10

Describe Characters' Responses
Reading: Literature

DIRECTIONS: Read the story. Then, answer the questions.

Strategy While reading, look for clue words after dialogue like *he said*, *replied*, and characters' names to know who is speaking. Try to see and hear the characters in your mind.

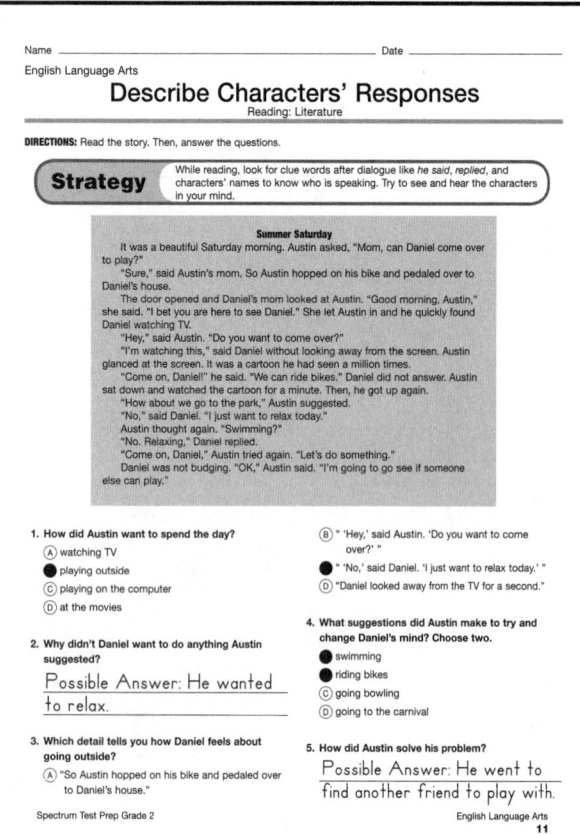

Summer Saturday

It was a beautiful Saturday morning. Austin asked, "Mom, can Daniel come over to play?"

"Sure," said Austin's mom. So Austin hopped on his bike and pedaled over to Daniel's house.

The door opened and Daniel's mom looked at Austin. "Good morning, Austin," she said. "I bet you are here to see Daniel." She let Austin in and he quickly found Daniel watching TV.

"Hey," said Austin. "Do you want to come over?"

"I'm watching this," said Daniel without looking away from the screen. Austin glanced at the screen. It was a cartoon he had seen a million times. "Come on, Daniel!" he said. "We can ride bikes." Daniel did not answer. Austin sat down and watched the cartoon for a minute. Then, he got up again.

"How about we go to the park," Austin suggested.

"No," said Daniel. "I just want to relax today."

Austin thought again. "Swimming?"

"No. Relaxing," Daniel replied.

"Come on, Daniel," Austin tried again. "Let's do something."

Daniel was not budging. "OK," Austin said. "I'm going to go see if someone else can play."

1. How did Austin want to spend the day?
(A) watching TV
● playing outside
(C) playing on the computer
(D) at the movies

2. Why didn't Daniel want to do anything Austin suggested?
<u>Possible Answer: He wanted</u> <u>to relax.</u>

3. Which detail tells you how Daniel feels about going outside?
(A) "So Austin hopped on his bike and pedaled over to Daniel's house."

(B) " 'Hey,' said Austin. 'Do you want to come over?' "
● " 'No,' said Daniel. 'I just want to relax today.' "
(D) "Daniel looked away from the TV for a second."

4. What suggestions did Austin make to try and change Daniel's mind? Choose two.
● swimming
● riding bikes
(C) going bowling
(D) going to the carnival

5. How did Austin solve his problem?
<u>Possible Answer: He went to</u> <u>find another friend to play with.</u>

11

Characters' Responses
Reading: Literature

1. Why did Ant gather food all year?
● so he would have food in the winter
(B) because he was always hungry
(C) to share it with the other insects
(D) so no other insects would have food

2. At the beginning of the story, what was Grasshopper's opinion about gathering food?
<u>Possible Answer: He thought</u> <u>the ant was being silly.</u>

3. What happened to Grasshopper when winter came?
<u>Possible Answer: He had no</u> <u>food. He was hungry.</u>

4. How did Ant feel when Grasshopper came to him for food?
(A) he was happy to help
● he didn't want to help, because he wanted Grasshopper to learn a lesson
(C) he didn't want to help, because he didn't want to share his food
(D) he didn't want to help, because Grasshopper was mean

5. What lessons do you think this story teaches?
<u>Possible Answer: I think that</u> <u>this story teaches that if you</u> <u>work hard and plan ahead, you</u> <u>will be able to enjoy life.</u>

13

Understand Poetry
Reading: Literature

DIRECTIONS: Read the poem. Then, answer the questions using key details from the poem.

Strategy Read each stanza, or part, of the poem carefully. Ask and answer the question *What is this stanza about?* before moving on to the next stanza.

Test Tip Read the poem quietly to yourself. Listen for the rhythm and rhyme of the words as you read.

From "The Arrow and the Song" by Henry W. Longfellow

I shot an arrow into the air,
It fell to earth, I do not know where;
It flew so fast that my sight
Could not follow it in its flight.

I sang a song into the air,
It fell to earth, I do not know where;
Because who has sight so sharp and strong
That it can follow the flight of song?

Long, long after, in an oak
I found the arrow, it had not broke;
And the song, from beginning to end,
I found again in the heart of a friend.

1. A rhyme pattern tells which words at the end of a line rhyme. What lines rhyme in stanza 1?
(A) 1 and 3
● 1 and 2; 3 and 4
(C) 1 and 4
(D) none

2. Write the pairs of rhyming words the poet uses.

Stanza 1: <u>air</u> <u>where</u>
<u>sight</u> <u>flight</u>

Stanza 2: <u>air</u> <u>where</u>
<u>strong</u> <u>song</u>

Stanza 3: <u>oak</u> <u>broke</u>
<u>end</u> <u>friend</u>

3. How are poems organized differently from stories?
<u>Possible Answer: Stories are organized</u>
<u>into paragraphs and sentences. Poems</u>
<u>are organized into stanzas and lines.</u>

4. Reread the first stanza. Write a sentence that describes what happens in that stanza.
<u>Possible Answer: The poet shot</u>
<u>an arrow. It flew so fast, he could</u>
<u>not see where it went.</u>

5. What did the poet send into the air in the second stanza?
● a song
(B) an arrow
(C) a friend
(D) an oak

Write how you know.
<u>Answer: The first line in the</u>
<u>stanza says I sang a song into</u>
<u>the air.</u>

14

Understand Poetry
Reading: Literature

DIRECTIONS: Read each poem. Then, answer the questions using key details from the poem.

Strategy As you read, mark the lines that rhyme.

Sweets, sweets are fun to eat
But too much yummy
can rot your teeth
and hurt your tummy

6. What rhyming words are in this poem?
<u>eat/teeth</u>
<u>yummy/tummy</u>

7. What message is the poet trying to tell you?
(A) Sweets are fun to eat.
(B) You should eat sweets every day.
● Sweets taste good, but aren't good for you.
(D) Brush your teeth each day or you will get cavities.

Allison the alligator
Absolutely adored acrobats.
Allison always attended any acrobatic affair
And as the acrobats ascended above
Allison always asked,
"How do I get up there?"

8. What is repeated in this poem?
(A) the word alligator
● the short a sound
(C) rhyming words
(D) the *ing* sound

Hey diddle, diddle
The cat and the fiddle,
The cow jumped over the moon.
The little dog laughed
To see such sport,
And the dish ran away with the spoon.

9. How is the last line of the poem different from the others?
<u>It does not have the</u>
<u>repeated sound.</u>

10. List the rhyming words from the poem.
<u>diddle</u> <u>fiddle</u>
<u>moon</u> <u>spoon</u>

11. How do the nonsense words "diddle diddle" affect this poem? Choose two.
● You know from the first line that it's a silly poem.
(B) The words make the poem more realistic.
● Silly words make a poem fun to read.
(D) Nonsense words always rhyme.

15

Describe Parts of a Story
Reading: Literature

DIRECTIONS: Read the story. Then, answer the questions using key details from the story.

Lazy Time

Sally and Ned are swaying slowly in the family swing. The air is crisp. Sally puts her arm around Ned and snuggles into his shaggy body. Ned's tongue licks Sally's hand that lies on her blue-jeaned leg. They watch a slow ladybug crawl underneath a pile of old, brown leaves. One red leaf drifts to the top of the ladybug's leaf pile. Ned's graying ears stand up as a *V* of geese honks goodbye. The sky slowly turns from blue, to pink, to purple, to black.

The first star shines as Sally's mom calls her in to eat. Sally gives a last push as she slides out of the swing. She walks to the back door of the house. Ned leaps down. He barks once at a rabbit and chases after Sally. She smiles and rubs Ned's head as they walk into the warm house together.

Strategy Most stories have the same parts: characters, settings, and events. As you read, identify these parts and make a list of each one.

Test Tip Details, especially ones that use the five senses, help you picture a story more clearly in your mind. Look for these details to understand the story.

1. The setting is _____.
(A) the main problem in a story
● where and when a story takes place
(C) the reason the author wrote a story
(D) the picture with a story

2. This story most likely takes place in _____.
(A) a made-up time
(B) the past
● the present
(D) the future

Write how you know.

Possible Answer: The details describe events that could take place today.

3. Write two key details that tell you that the story takes place in the autumn.

Possible Answer: The air is crisp. Ned's graying ears stand up as a V of geese honks goodbye.

4. What do the details tell you about Ned?

Possible Answer: That he is a dog.

5. What does the beginning of the story introduce?
● It introduces the characters.
(B) It describes the setting.
(C) It describes the plot of the story.
(D) It tells how the story ends.

16

Describe Parts of a Story
Reading: Literature

DIRECTIONS: Read the story. Then, answer the questions using key details from the story.

Strategy As you read, identify the problem the characters face. Write the problem down. Then, find details that tell how the characters solve the problem.

Skating

It was a sunny, spring day. Jason could not wait for Tasha to show him how to use his new inline skates. Jason had always wanted skates. He finally got them for his birthday. Now, he was ready for his first lesson. Jason and Tasha went to the park.

When they got to the park, they saw Michael. Michael raced by the slower skaters and made a face at them. "Show-off," Jason said.

Suddenly, Jason heard a loud crash on the other side of the park.

"What was that?" asked Tasha.

Michael limped around the corner. He was covered with twigs and leaves.

"I don't think we have to worry about show-offs anymore," Jason said with a smile.

1. Describe the setting of the story.

Possible Answer: The setting is a park on a sunny, spring day.

2. Who are the two main characters in the story?
(A) Michael and Tasha
(B) Jason and Michael
● Jason and Tasha
(D) the skates

Write how you know.

Possible Answer: Michael is in the story, but the story is mainly about Tasha and Jason.

Test Tip
A story has a beginning, a middle, and an end. The problem is usually told in the beginning and solved by the end.

3. How does the beginning introduce the story?

Possible Answer: The beginning tells the setting and the characters. It explains why Jason is going to the park with Tasha.

4. Which key detail tells you the problem in the story?
(A) "Jason had always wanted skates."
(B) "Jason and Tasha went to the park."
● "Michael raced by the slower skaters and made a face at them."
(D) "Michael limped around the corner."

5. Why did Jason smile at the end of the story? How was his problem solved?
(A) Jason was a good skater.
(B) Tasha went home.
(C) Michael raced past them.
● Michael would not be showing off anymore.

17

Compare and Contrast
Reading: Literature

DIRECTIONS: Read the stories. Then, answer the questions.

Strategy Read to identify details that are similar and details that are different between two stories. Ask yourself, *How are the characters, settings, and events of the stories alike? How are they different?*

Adapted from Snow White

Snow White's stepmother was a wicked woman. But, she was also very beautiful. The magic mirror told her this every day, whenever she asked it. "Mirror, mirror on the wall, who is the loveliest of all?" The reply was always; "You are, your Majesty." The awful day came when she heard it say, "Snow White is the loveliest of all."

The stepmother was angry and wild with jealousy. She began plotting to get rid of Snow White. She bribed one of her trusty servants with a rich reward to take Snow White into the forest far away from the castle. Then, he was to put her to death. The greedy servant was attracted to the reward. He agreed to do this deed and led the innocent little girl away. However, the man's courage failed him. Leaving Snow White sitting beside a tree, he mumbled an excuse and ran off.

Snow White was alone in the dark forest. She began to cry bitterly. She heard strange sounds and rustlings that made her heart thump. At last, overcome by tiredness, she fell asleep curled under a tree.

Adapted from The Story of Princess Hase-Hime (a Japanese fairy tale)

There was only one person who was not pleased by Princess Hase-Hime, and that was her stepmother. She had the embarrassment of seeing her stepdaughter rise to power and honor. The young girl was favored and admired by the whole Court. The stepmother's envy and jealousy burned in her heart like fire. She created many lies to tell her husband about Hase-Hime. He would not believe her tales and sharply told her she was wrong.

At last her husband went on a trip to a far-off land. The stepmother ordered one of her old servants to take the innocent Hase-Hime to the Hibari Mountains. This was the wildest part of the country. She told the old man to kill the girl there. The servant could not disobey. But, he knew the young girl was innocent of all the things her stepmother had invented. He was determined to save the girl. Unless he killed her however, he could not return to his cruel ruler. So, he made up his mind to stay in the wilderness with the young princess and keep her safe.

1. Write the phrases and words below in the Venn diagram to compare and contrast the two stories.

beautiful	woods	mountains	wicked stepmother
anger and jealousy	plot to kill girl	magic mirror	bribed servant
servant did not kill girl	left girl alone	stayed with girl	ordered servant
favored and admired			

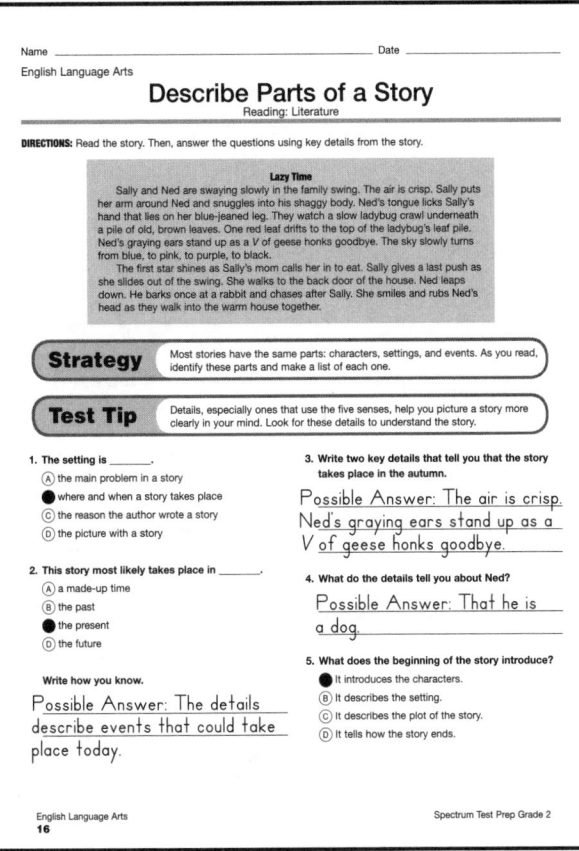

Snow White | Both | Hase-Hime
beautiful / woods / magic mirror / bribed servant / left girl alone
wicked stepmother / anger and jealousy / plot to kill girl / servant did not kill girl
mountains / stayed with girl / ordered servant / favored and admired

18

Compare and Contrast
Reading: Literature

Strategy Draw a chart or diagram to organize the characters, setting, and events in each story. A Venn diagram can help you see details that are the same and details that are different.

Test Tip Read each question carefully to decide if it is asking you about one story or both stories.

2. Why did Snow White's stepmother want her killed?
(A) Everyone favored and admired Snow White.
(B) Snow White was not a real princess.
● Snow White was more beautiful.
(D) She wanted Snow White's money.

Write how you know.

Possible Answer: Snow White's stepmother asked a magic mirror who was the most beautiful. When the mirror said Snow White was the most beautiful, the stepmother planned to get rid of Snow White.

3. Why did Hase-Hime's stepmother want her killed?

Possible Answer: The stepmother was jealous of Hase-Hime.

Write how you know.

Possible Answer: The passage states "The stepmother's envy and jealousy burned in her heart like fire."

4. Which key details helped you answer question 3? Choose two.
● "She had the embarrassment of seeing her stepdaughter rise to power and honor."
● "The stepmother's envy and jealousy burned in her heart like fire."
(C) "At last her husband went on a trip to a far-off land."
(D) "The servant could not disobey."

Test Tip
When comparing two stories, be sure to look for what is the same and for what is different.

5. Use what you wrote in the Venn diagram to write a sentence that shows how the two stories are alike.

Possible Answer: In both stories, a wicked stepmother is jealous of her stepdaughter and tries to have her killed.

6. Use what you wrote in the Venn diagram to write a sentence that shows how the two stories are different.

Possible Answer: In Snow White, the servant left the girl alone in the woods. In Hase-Hime, the servant stayed with the girl to keep her safe.

19

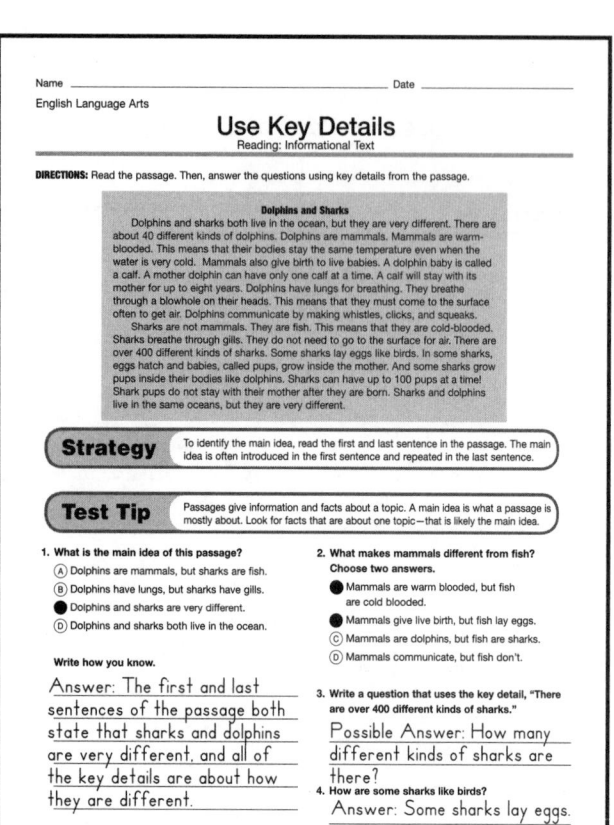

Page 20

Use Key Details
Reading: Informational Text

DIRECTIONS: Read the passage. Then, answer the questions using key details from the passage.

Dolphins and Sharks

Dolphins and sharks both live in the ocean, but they are very different. There are about 40 different kinds of dolphins. Dolphins are mammals. Mammals are warm-blooded. This means that their bodies stay the same temperature even when the water is very cold. Mammals also give birth to live babies. A dolphin baby is called a calf. A mother dolphin can have only one calf at a time. A calf will stay with its mother for up to eight years. Dolphins have lungs for breathing. They breathe through a blowhole on their heads. This means that they must come to the surface often to get air. Dolphins communicate by making whistles, clicks, and squeaks.

Sharks are not mammals. They are fish. This means that they are cold-blooded. Sharks breathe through gills. They do not need to go to the surface for air. There are over 400 different kinds of sharks. Some sharks lay eggs like birds. In some sharks, eggs hatch and babies, called pups, grow inside the mother. And some sharks grow pups inside their bodies like dolphins. Sharks can have up to 100 pups at a time! Shark pups do not stay with their mother after they are born. Sharks and dolphins live in the same oceans, but they are very different.

Strategy — To identify the main idea, read the first and last sentence in the passage. The main idea is often introduced in the first sentence and repeated in the last sentence.

Test Tip — Passages give information and facts about a topic. A main idea is what a passage is mostly about. Look for facts that are about one topic—that is likely the main idea.

1. What is the main idea of this passage?
- (A) Dolphins are mammals, but sharks are fish.
- (B) Dolphins have lungs, but sharks have gills.
- ● Dolphins and sharks are very different.
- (D) Dolphins and sharks both live in the ocean.

Write how you know.

Answer: The first and last sentences of the passage both state that sharks and dolphins are very different, and all of the key details are about how they are different.

2. What makes mammals different from fish? Choose two answers.
- ● Mammals are warm blooded, but fish are cold blooded.
- ● Mammals give live birth, but fish lay eggs.
- (C) Mammals are dolphins, but fish are sharks.
- (D) Mammals communicate, but fish don't.

3. Write a question that uses the key detail, "There are over 400 different kinds of sharks."

Possible Answer: How many different kinds of sharks are there?

4. How are some sharks like birds?

Answer: Some sharks lay eggs.

Page 21

Use Key Details
Reading: Informational Text

DIRECTIONS: Read the passage. Then, answer the questions using key details from the passage.

India

In the United States, most people speak English. In India, there are more than 1,000 different languages. This has caused many problems. Many of the people speak the words in different ways. Hindi was chosen as the main language to solve the problem. However, it is still hard for people to talk to each other.

There are many ways to let others know what you think without using words. Some actions mean different things in India. For example, to show an older person that you respect him, bow down and touch his feet. If you want to be rude, sit with the bottoms of your shoes showing. To show you are clean, never wear your shoes in the house. If you don't want to be polite, point at your feet.

Strategy — Write the main idea down and then list 2 or 3 key details that support it.

Test Tip — A key detail tells more information about the main idea. Key details support the main idea of the story.

5. What is the main idea of the passage?
- (A) It is fun to live in India.
- (B) Learning to read is important.
- (C) Never point at your feet or show the bottom of your shoes.
- ● In India, there are many ways to let others know what you think without words.

Which sentence helps you identify the main idea?

Answer: There are many ways to let others know what you think without using words.

6. Based on the passage, what is rude in India?
- (A) never wearing your shoes in the house
- (B) learning how to read
- ● sitting with the bottoms of your shoes showing
- (D) going to the store

Write how you know.

Possible Answer: A key detail is if you want to be rude, sit with the bottoms of your shoes showing.

7. Write a question that uses the key detail, ". . . bow down and touch an older person's feet."

Possible Answer: How do you show an older person respect in India?

Write how you know.

Possible Answer: The detail in the passage says "For example, to show an older person that you respect him, bow down and touch his feet."

8. In India, how would a person show he or she is clean?
- (A) They point to their feet.
- (B) They bow down and touch your feet.
- ● They do not wear shoes in the house.
- (D) They show the bottoms of their shoes.

Page 22

Find Word Meanings
Reading: Informational Text

DIRECTIONS: Read the passage. Then, answer the questions.

Horses are beautiful animals. Most horses have smooth, shiny coats. They have long manes and tails. Their hair may be brown, black, white, yellow, or spotted. Sometimes, horses neigh, or make a loud, long cry. Horses need to be groomed, or brushed, every day. This helps keep them clean. Many people keep horses as pets or to work on farms. Some people enjoy riding them for fun. Horses are wonderful animals.

Strategy — Circle words in the passage that you do not know. Then, read the passage and draw boxes around words in the passage that help you find the meaning of the unknown words.

Test Tip — When you come across a new word, use the words around it to help you find its meaning.

1. What does the word neigh mean?
- ● make a loud, long cry
- (B) no
- (C) whistle loudly
- (D) talk in horse language

2. What might a spotted horse look like?

Possible Answer: A spotted horse might be brown with white spots.

3. What is another word for groomed?
- (A) loud
- (B) worked
- ● brushed
- (D) spotted

Test Tip

When comparing two stories, be sure to look for what is the same and for what is different.

DIRECTIONS: Read the sentences. Then, choose the word that fits in both sentences.

4. _____ to the left.
The _____ on this pencil broke.
- ● point
- (B) eraser
- (C) shine
- (D) top

5. The boat began to _____.
Dad washed the dishes in the _____.
- (A) wait
- (B) tub
- ● sink
- (D) pan

6. Hit the _____ with the hammer.
The _____ on my little finger is broken.
- (A) tack
- ● nail
- (C) skin
- (D) wood

Page 23

Find Word Meanings
Reading: Informational Text

DIRECTIONS: Read the sentences. Then, choose the word that means the same as the underlined word.

Strategy — Use the general meaning of the sentence to find the meaning of unknown words. The unknown word should connect, or relate, to what is happening in the sentence.

Test Tip — Try each word in place of the underlined word in the sentence.

7. Jane's mom wrote a memo about her daughter's illness to the teacher.
- ● message
- (B) drink
- (C) pencil
- (D) ticket

8. Susan was grateful that her dad drove her to school because it was raining.
- ● thankful
- (B) sad
- (C) angry
- (D) finished

Write how you know.

Possible Answer: The other choices do not make sense in the sentence. Susan would not be sad or angry that she didn't have to walk in the rain. She also did not do anything in the sentence to finish.

9. The brothers bellowed for their dog to come home.
- (A) cared
- ● yelled
- (C) heard
- (D) whispered

10. Grandma asked me to divide the cookies evenly between the children.
- (A) use
- (B) bake
- ● split
- (D) stand

Write how you know.

Possible Answer: The word evenly tells me that the word split makes sense in the sentence. The word split connects to what is happening in the sentence. You can split cookies evenly.

11. I always keep my room immaculate. Everything is in its place.
- (A) bad
- (B) pretty
- ● clean
- (D) dark

12. The Grand Canyon is an immense hole in the ground.
- ● huge
- (B) tiny
- (C) ready
- (D) round

Describe Connections
Reading: Informational Text

DIRECTIONS: Read the passage. Then, answer the questions using key details from the passage.

How to Make a Peanut Butter and Jelly Sandwich
You will need peanut butter, jelly, and two pieces of bread. First, spread peanut butter on one piece of bread. Next, spread jelly on the other piece. Then, put the two pieces of bread together. Next, cut the sandwich in half. Finally, eat your sandwich and enjoy!

Strategy Number each step of the process in order (1, 2, 3) to make sure you understand the sequence, or order, of the process.

Test Tip Words like *first, next,* and *finally* are clues to the order of the steps.

1. What is this paragraph explaining?
ⓐ how to make peanut butter
ⓑ how to cut a sandwich
● how to make a peanut butter and jelly sandwich
ⓓ how to put bread together

Write how you know: Possible Answer: The title is "How to Make a Peanut Butter and Jelly Sandwich."

2. What does the paragraph say to do after you spread peanut butter on one piece of bread?
Spread jelly on the other piece of bread.

3. Why is the first sentence important?
Possible Answer: It tells you what you need to make the sandwich.

Can you take out the first sentence? Why or why not?
Possible Answer: No. If the first sentence were taken out, you would not know what to use to make the sandwich.

4. What is the last step in the paragraph?
ⓐ Put the two pieces of bread together.
ⓑ Cut the sandwich.
● Eat and enjoy your sandwich.
ⓓ Spread peanut butter on one piece of bread.

5. What would happen if you put the two pieces of bread together before spreading the jelly?
Possible Answer: You would have jelly on the outside of your sandwich.

Write how you know.
Possible Answer: The passage says to spread jelly on a piece of bread before putting the bread together.

6. Which step could you leave out if you wanted to?
ⓐ Spread the peanut butter.
ⓑ Spread the jelly.
ⓒ Put the two pieces of bread together.
● Cut the sandwich in half.

24

Describe Connections
Reading: Informational Text

DIRECTIONS: Read the passage.

Insects in Winter
In the summertime, insects can be seen buzzing and fluttering around us. But as winter's cold weather begins, the insects seem to disappear. Do you know where they go? Many insects find a warm place to spend the winter.
Ants try to dig deep into the ground. Some beetles stack up in piles under rocks or dead leaves.
Female grasshoppers do not even stay around for winter. In the fall, they lay their eggs and die. The eggs hatch in the spring.
Bees also try to protect themselves from the winter cold. Honeybees gather in a ball in the middle of their hive. The bees form this tight ball trying to stay warm.
Winter is very hard for insects, but each spring the survivors come out, and the buzzing and fluttering begin again.

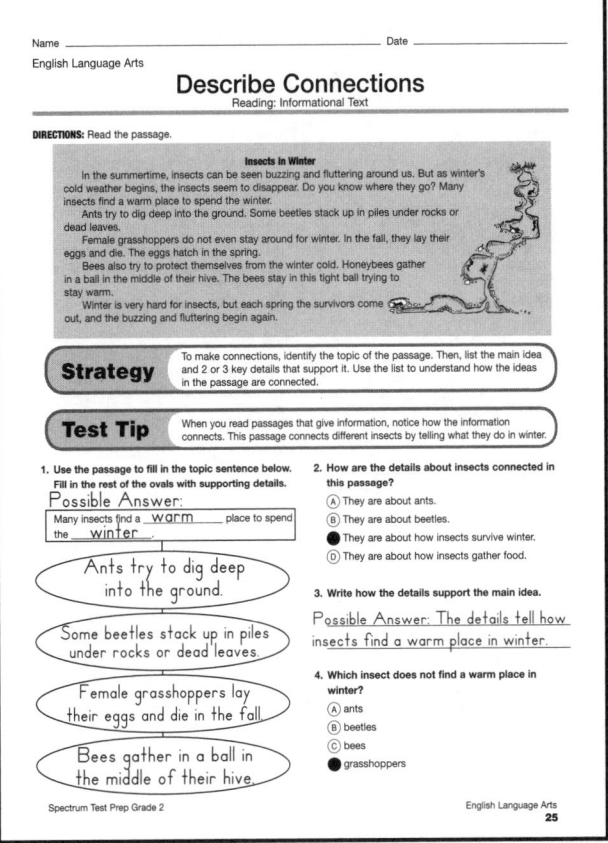

Strategy To make connections, identify the topic of the passage. Then, list the main idea and 2 or 3 key details that support it. Use the list to understand how the ideas in the passage are connected.

Test Tip When you read passages that give information, notice how the information connects. This passage connects different insects by telling what they do in winter.

1. Use the passage to fill in the topic sentence below. Fill in the rest of the ovals with supporting details.
Possible Answer:
Many insects find a **warm** place to spend the **winter**.

Ants try to dig deep into the ground.

Some beetles stack up in piles under rocks or dead leaves.

Female grasshoppers lay their eggs and die in the fall.

Bees gather in a ball in the middle of their hive.

2. How are the details about insects connected in this passage?
ⓐ They are about ants.
ⓑ They are about beetles.
● They are about how insects survive winter.
ⓓ They are about how insects gather food.

3. Write how the details support the main idea.
Possible Answer: The details tell how insects find a warm place in winter.

4. Which insect does not find a warm place in winter?
ⓐ ants
ⓑ beetles
ⓒ bees
● grasshoppers

25

Identify Author's Purpose
Reading: Informational Text

DIRECTIONS: Read the passage. Then, answer the questions using key details from the passage.

Therapy Dogs
Dogs can help people get better after they've been sick. These special dogs are called therapy dogs.
The dogs' owners bring them into hospital rooms. They let people meet the dogs. Sometimes, the dogs go right up to the beds. People can pet the dogs, brush them, and talk to them. Studies have shown that being with dogs and other animals can help people heal faster.
Not every dog is a good choice for this important job. A therapy dog must be calm and friendly. Some therapy dog owners feel that their pets were born to help sick people get well again.

Strategy While you read a detail in the passage, ask yourself *Why did the author include this detail? What is the author trying to tell me as a reader?*

Test Tip The author's purpose is the reason he or she wrote a passage. Authors often write passages to give information.

1. Which sentence best summarizes the author's main point?
ⓐ Therapy dogs like to be brushed.
ⓑ Therapy dogs are calm and friendly.
● Therapy dogs help sick people get better.
ⓓ Therapy dogs enjoy visiting people in hospitals.

Write how you know. Which sentence in the passage supports this as the main idea?
Dogs can help people get better after they've been sick.

2. Choose two details to support the author's claim that not every dog is a good choice to be a therapy dog.
ⓐ "Sometimes, the dogs go right up to the beds."
● "A therapy dog must be calm and friendly."
ⓒ "People can pet the dogs, brush them, and talk to them."
● "Some therapy dog owners feel that their pets were born to help sick people get well again."

3. Write the reason the author wrote this passage.
Possible Answers: to explain what therapy dogs do; to give information about therapy dogs

4. Would an excited and unfriendly dog make a good therapy dog? Write how you know.
Possible Answer: No. The text says that a therapy dog must be calm and friendly.

5. Write the sentence that tells how therapy dogs help sick people.
People can pet the dogs, brush them, and talk to them.

6. Where could you look to find more information about therapy dogs?
ⓐ a website about types of dogs
● a website about helper animals
ⓒ the dictionary
ⓓ a map

26

Identify Author's Purpose
Reading: Informational Text

DIRECTIONS: Read the passage. Then, answer the questions.

Jellyfish
Jellyfish come in all sizes and colors. Some are only one inch across. Other jellyfish are five feet wide. Some are orange. Others are red. Some jellyfish have no color at all. Gently poke one type of jellyfish with a stick, and it will glow. However, do not let any jellyfish touch you, because they can sting!

Strategy While reading, identify the main idea of a passage. Use the main idea to find the author's purpose, or what information the author wants to share with readers.

Test Tip Key details support the author's main idea.

7. Which sentence best summarizes the author's main point?
ⓐ Jellyfish can sting.
● There are many kinds of jellyfish.
ⓒ Some jellyfish are orange.
ⓓ Jellyfish can hide.

Write the sentence that tells you the main point.
Jellyfish come in all sizes and colors.

8. Write two key details that support the author's main point.
Possible Answer: Some are only one inch across. Some jellyfish have no color at all.

9. Why did the author write this passage?
ⓐ To give an opinion about jellyfish.
ⓑ To explain how jellyfish sting.
● To describe different kinds of jellyfish.
ⓓ To tell a story with jellyfish as characters.

Write how you know.
Possible Answer: All of the details tell about different kinds of jellyfish.

10. Write the key detail that supports the author's claim that you should never touch a jellyfish.
However, do not let any jellyfish touch you, because they can sting!

11. Choose two facts the author used to support the idea that jellyfish come in all sizes.
● Some are only one inch across.
● Other jellyfish are five feet wide.
ⓒ Some are orange.
ⓓ Others are red.

12. How would the passage change if the author did not use facts to support the main point?
Possible Answer: The main point would not be supported. The main point would not be a fact.

27

Name _____ Date _____
English Language Arts

Use Text Features
Reading: Informational Text

DIRECTIONS: Write or choose the correct answer.

Strategy Use text features such as the table of contents, glossary, illustrations, and headings to find information. Read the text feature carefully to know what kind of information is given.

Test Tip When you are putting words in alphabetical order, look at the next letter in the word if the first letters are the same.

1. Which set of words is in the order they would appear in a glossary?
● Ⓐ cat, dog, light, star
Ⓑ dog, cat, light, star
Ⓒ star, light, cat, dog
Ⓓ light, cat, star, dog

Write how you know.

Possible Answer: The words are in alphabetical order.

2. The guide words at the top of your glossary page are "face–fish." Which word will you find on the page?
Ⓐ full
Ⓑ time
Ⓒ enough
● Ⓓ factory

Write how you know.

Possible Answer: I used alphabetical order. The word factory comes after the word face and before the word fish.

3. Which heading would you look under to find out what sharks eat?
Ⓐ Sharks Are Everywhere
Ⓑ A Shark's Body
● Ⓒ Dinner Time!
Ⓓ Predator Or Prey?

DIRECTIONS: Use the Table of Contents and Index to answer questions 4 and 5.

TABLE OF CONTENTS		INDEX	
Painting	3	colors	8, 22, 31
Drawing	14	museums	2, 10, 19, 35
Index	53	pencil	16
Glossary	57	watercolor paints	5

4. On what page does the chapter on drawing start?
Ⓐ page 3
● Ⓑ page 14
Ⓒ page 53
Ⓓ page 57

5. If you wanted to learn the meaning of the word docent, which page would you turn to?

57

Write how you know.

Possible Answer: If I want to know the meaning of a word, I would need to look in the glossary, which starts on page 57.

English Language Arts
28

Spectrum Test Prep Grade 2

Name _____ Date _____
English Language Arts

Use Text Features
Reading: Informational Text

DIRECTIONS: Read the passage. Then, answer the questions.

Strategy Look at illustrations and other images carefully and compare the information in the illustration to the information in the passage. Is there new information in the image? Or does it match information in the passage?

Signing
People who may not be able to hear or speak well use sign language. They use their hands instead of their voices to talk. Their hands make signals to show different letters, words, and ideas. For example, to say the word love, cross your arms over your chest.

Other people use sign language, too. Have you ever watched a football game? The referees use hand signals to let you know what has happened in the game, such as a foul or time-out. Have you ever watched a police officer direct traffic? The police officer can use sign language to tell cars to stop and go.

Guess who else uses sign language? You! You wave your hand when you say hello and good-bye. You nod your head up and down to say yes. You shake your head back and forth to say no. You use your fingers to point and show which way to go. We use our hands and body to make signals all of the time!

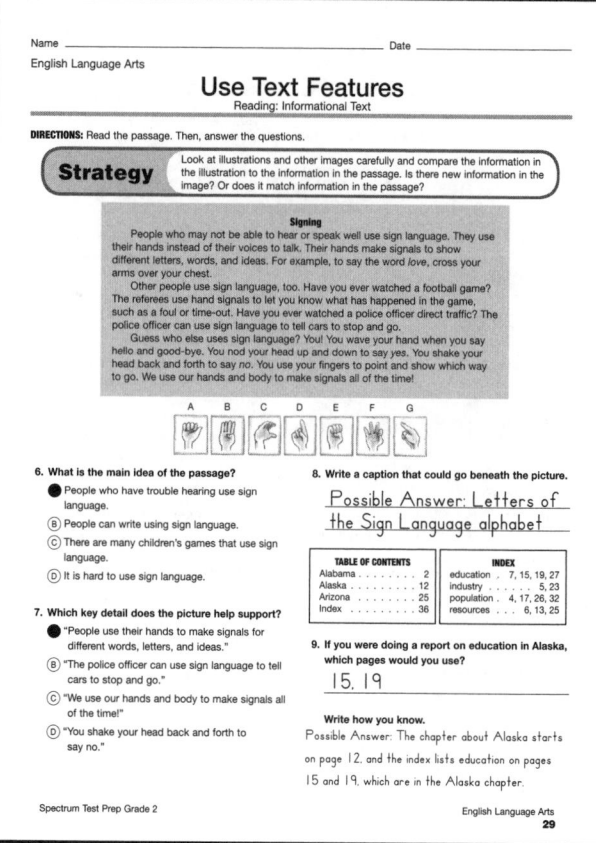

6. What is the main idea of the passage?
● Ⓐ People who have trouble hearing use sign language.
Ⓑ People can write using sign language.
Ⓒ There are many children's games that use sign language.
Ⓓ It is hard to use sign language.

7. Which key detail does the picture help support?
● Ⓐ "People use their hands to make signals for different words, letters, and ideas."
Ⓑ "The police officer can use sign language to tell cars to stop and go."
Ⓒ "We use our hands and body to make signals all of the time!"
Ⓓ "You shake your head back and forth to say no."

8. Write a caption that could go beneath the picture.

Possible Answer: Letters of the Sign Language alphabet

TABLE OF CONTENTS		INDEX	
Alabama	3	education	7, 15, 19, 27
Alaska	12	industry	5, 23
Arizona	25	population	4, 17, 26, 32
Index	36	resources	6, 13, 25

9. If you were doing a report on education in Alaska, which pages would you use?

15, 19

Write how you know.

Possible Answer: The chapter about Alaska starts on page 12, and the index lists education on pages 15 and 19, which are in the Alaska chapter.

Spectrum Test Prep Grade 2

English Language Arts
29

Name _____ Date _____
English Language Arts

Compare Two Passages
Reading: Informational Text

DIRECTIONS: Read the passages. Then, answer the questions.

Strategy When you read two passages on the same topic, identify details that are the same and details that are different. Underline details that are the same in both passages. Circle details that are different.

Teachers Learn
To be a teacher, you have to be very smart. You have to learn and be able to teach about almost anything. Teachers work very hard. They plan lessons, grade papers, write report cards, and help students with their work. Some teachers teach only one subject. Other teachers teach many different subjects. Teaching is a very hard job.

Teachers Care
To be a teacher, you have to be very caring. You have to support children and be able to help them learn almost anything. Teachers work very hard. They plan for students to be successful. They get to read all of the interesting things children write. They help children become better learners. Some teachers teach only a few children. Other teachers teach many children. Teaching is a very rewarding job.

1. Both passages are about teaching, but how are they different? Use the T-chart to list key ideas from both passages that show these differences.

The author of passage 1 thinks that teachers . . .	The author of passage 2 thinks that teachers . . .
Possible Answers: have to be smart; plan lessons; grade papers; write report cards; help students do their work; teach one or many subjects	Possible Answers: have to be caring; plan for student success; get to read student work; support children and help them learn; help children become better learners; teach few or many children

2. How are these two passages alike?
Ⓐ They both tell how teaching is a hard job.
Ⓑ They both tell how teaching is a rewarding job.
● Ⓒ They both tell how teachers work hard.
Ⓓ They both tell how teachers plan lessons.

3. Both passages tell about teachers, but each has a different focus. What is the focus of the first passage?

Possible Answer: The work teachers do.

What is the focus of the second passage?

Possible Answer: How teachers help children learn.

English Language Arts
30

Spectrum Test Prep Grade 2

Name _____ Date _____
English Language Arts

Compare Two Passages
Reading: Informational Text

DIRECTIONS: Read the passages. Then, answer the questions.

Strategy When comparing two passages, identify and write down the topic of each passage. Then, write the main idea of each topic. Are the main ideas the same? Are they different?

Growing Dinner
Do you know where the food on your dinner table came from? It most likely came from a grocery store. But, what if you could grow your own dinner?

Planting and caring for a garden is an easy and fun thing to do. You first have to find a good spot for your garden. The spot should be sunny and protected from animals. You can use almost any container for gardening. Whether you put your garden in a container or dig it into the ground, you will need good soil.

Once you have your spot and your soil, you can plant your vegetables. You can start your vegetables from seeds or from small plants. Water your plants and pull the weeds. In a few weeks, you'll have some delicious vegetables. You can cook them up for dinner or eat them raw for a snack!

Gardening Fun
Gardening is a fun hobby. Many people enjoy the feeling of digging in the earth. Others enjoy the peace and quiet of being outside in nature. Whatever the reason, anybody can become a gardener.

Some people like to plant vegetables. Others like to plant flowers. The people who work at nurseries, or plant stores, will know which plants grow best where you live.

Once you know what you want to plant, you are on your way to becoming a gardener! Find a good, sunny spot. Put down some nice, rich soil. Bury your seeds, or put in your small plants. Then, all you have to do is water and pull out any weeds that grow. The insects and birds will love your garden as much as you do!

4. Write three important facts from the first passage, "Growing Dinner."

Possible Answer: You can use almost any container for gardening. You can start your vegetables from seeds or from small plants. In a few weeks you'll have some delicious vegetables.

5. Write two key details from "Gardening Fun" that support the main idea "Gardening is a fun hobby."

Possible Answer: Many people enjoy the feeling of digging in the earth. Others enjoy the peace and quiet of being outside in nature.

6. What are both passages mainly about?
Ⓐ the kinds of containers used for gardens
Ⓑ different types of gardens
● Ⓒ the joy of gardening
Ⓓ How to plant vegetables

7. Write three ideas that can be found in both passages.

Answer: Gardening is fun. Gardens should be in a good, sunny spot. Gardens need good soil. You have to take care of gardens.

Spectrum Test Prep Grade 2

English Language Arts
31

Use Nouns and Pronouns
Language

DIRECTIONS: Choose or write the correct answer.

Strategy — Identify the noun in a sentence. Then, to make sure you use the correct noun, ask yourself if the noun is singular (one), plural (more than one), or possessive (belongs to).

Test Tip — Some nouns change when they name more than one person, place, or thing. For example, child becomes children and mouse becomes mice.

1. Choose the sentence that is written correctly.
(A) My foots are so tired from walking!
(B) The childs played on the swings together.
● There were two mice under the stoop.
(D) Don't forget to brush your tooths.

2. Choose the sentence that is incorrect. Then, write it correctly.
(A) The children played at the park.
(B) I jumped more than two feet in the air!
● Caleb has lost three tooths already.
(D) Two mice ran across the field.

My correction:
Caleb has lost three teeth already.

3. Write the sentence correctly on the line.
The knife go in that drawer.
The knives go in that drawer.

Test Tip
A pronoun stands in for a noun. Some pronouns include *I, me, my, they, them, their, anyone, everything, myself, herself,* and *himself.* For singular nouns, use *he, she,* and *it.* For plural nouns, use *they* and *them.*

4. Choose the sentence that is written correctly.
● I gave myself a haircut!
(B) He got a new coat for hisself.
(C) I'm so excited, I can hardly control mineself.
(D) Yourself is really pretty.

5. Write the pronouns that replace the underlined words in the sentences.
Madelyn and Ryan study together.
Chris gave his math notes to Mike.
Sheri invited all of the students to the party.
They, him, everyone

6. Choose the sentence that is incorrect. Then, write it correctly.
(A) Aubrey and Ben stayed home by themselves.
(B) Addison and William made themselves lunch.
(C) Addison poured herself some milk.
● John went by theirself to the store.

My correction:
John went by himself to the store.

32

Use Nouns and Pronouns
Language

Strategy — Use singular pronouns to replace singular nouns. Use plural pronouns to replace plural nouns.

Test Tip — Look up nouns in a dictionary to learn their plural form.

7. Write the plural form of each word on the line.
tooth	teeth
woman	women
fly	flies
loaf	loaves

8. What do you call a group of
geese?	gaggle
fish?	school
flowers?	bouquet
cows?	herd

9. Write the correct pronoun on the line.
He went to the store by __himself__.

10. Write a sentence using the pronouns below.
she herself
She learned to read by herself.

11. Which nouns are replaced by the pronouns in the sentence below?
They built a fort all by themselves.
● Matt and Russ
(B) Boy
(C) Matt
(D) Russ

Write how you know.
Possible Answer: The pronouns *They* and *themselves* are used for more than one person.

33

Use Verbs
Language

DIRECTIONS: Read each sentence and choose or write the correct answer.

Strategy — Use the endings of verbs to identify if the action is happening now, in the past, or in the future.

Test Tip — Verbs can show if an action is happening now, in the past, or in the future. This is called verb tense. Learn how to form each type of verb. Some past tense verbs change spelling.

Present	Past	Future
walks	walked	will walk
sits	sat	will sit
hides	hid	will hide

Test Tip
Read each sentence carefully to find verb errors. Try reading sentences out loud to yourself to hear how they sound.

1. Choose the sentence that is written correctly.
(A) I sitted on the bench.
(B) Jose set on the grass.
● Angel sat on the swing.
(D) Jesse sit on the slide.

2. Write the sentence using the past tense of hide.
The squirrel hides his nuts behind the tree.
The squirrel hid his nuts behind the tree.

3. Choose the sentence that uses a verb in the future tense.
(A) My mom tell me a funny story.
(B) I told it to Sue.
● Sue will tell it to Cate.
(D) Cate tolded it to Victor.

4. Choose the sentence that is written correctly.
(A) Last summer, I swum at the beach.
(B) Yesterday, I swimmed in a pool.
● Last week, Abbie swam in a lake.
(D) Sam swamed in a river.

5. Choose the sentence that is incorrect. Then, write it correctly.
● Marco hitted the ball very hard.
(B) Luke sat in the back seat.
(C) Hannah hid in the closet.
(D) Mr. Jones runs three miles.

My correction:
Marco hit the ball very hard.

6. Choose the sentence that is incorrect. Then, write it correctly.
(A) We ate at a nice restaurant yesterday.
(B) They eat at home on Tuesdays.
(C) I eat at school every day.
● Ethan eated at his friend's house last week.

My correction:
Ethan ate at a friend's house.

34

Use Verbs
Language

DIRECTIONS: Read the sentence. Write the past tense of the verb correctly on the line.

Strategy — Try the verb in different tenses in the sentences. Read the sentences to yourself to see which word makes sense.

Test Tip — Remember that some verbs do not use *-ed* at the end when they are put into past tense. For example, the past tense of go is *went.* Some verbs don't change at all. The past tense of *let* is *let.*

7. Complete the chart with the correct verb tense.
Present	Past	Future
fly	flew	will fly
bend	bent	will bend
talk	talked	will talk
hop	hopped	will hop
see	saw	will see
snow	snowed	will snow

8. The dog __sat__ on the grass. (sit)

9. I __went__ to the mall yesterday. (go)

10. It __began__ to rain outside. (begin)

11. Sophie __held__ her breath for 15 seconds! (hold)

12. Kevin __hurt__ his leg playing soccer. (hurt)

13. Olivia __met__ a new friend yesterday. (meet)

14. Isabella __put__ a sticker on my paper. (put)

DIRECTIONS: Write a sentence that uses the past tense of the verb. Possible Answers:

15. ride
Yesterday,
I rode my scooter to school.

16. say
Last night,
Mom said she loved me.

17. dig
Last weekend,
we dug a garden.

18. bite
Yesterday,
I bit my tongue.

35

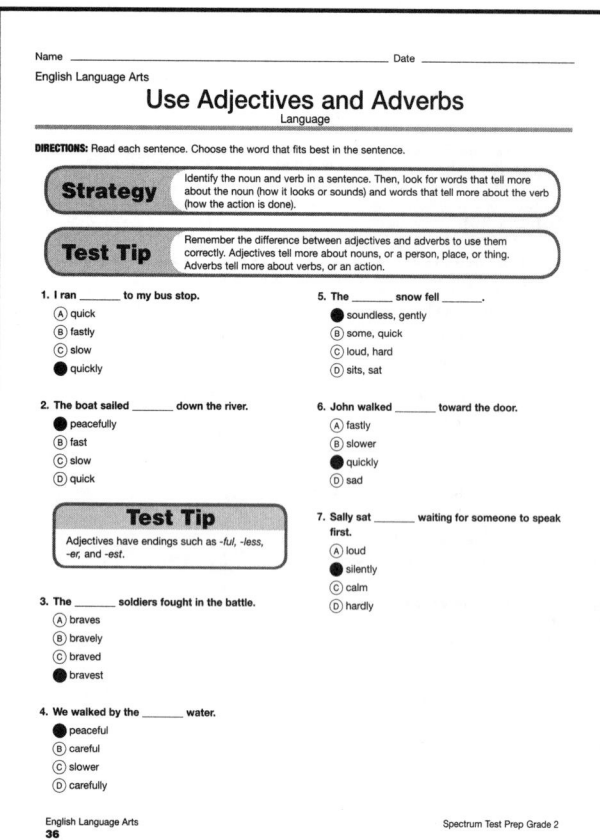

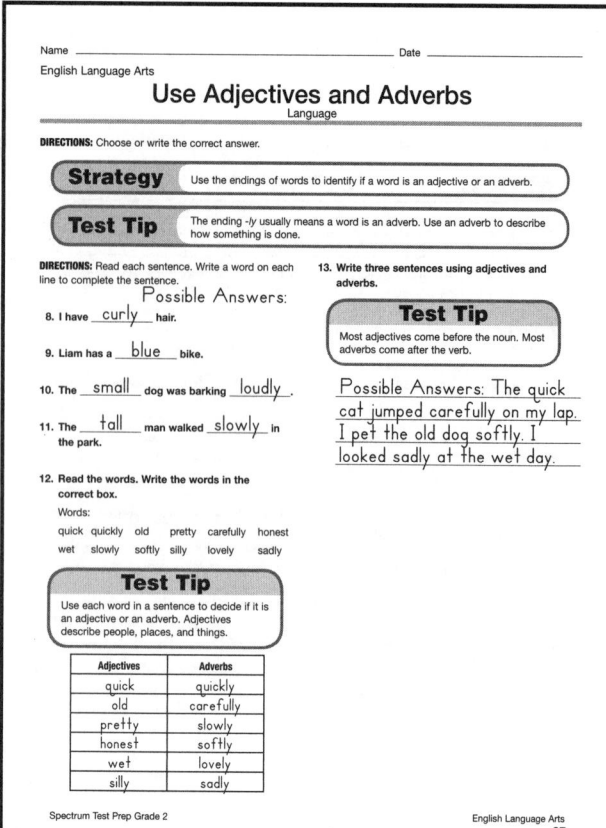

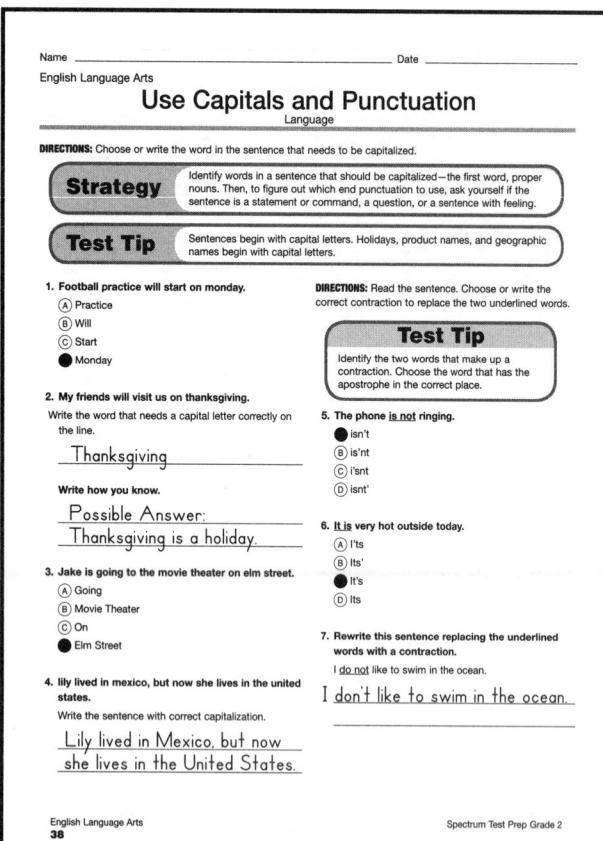

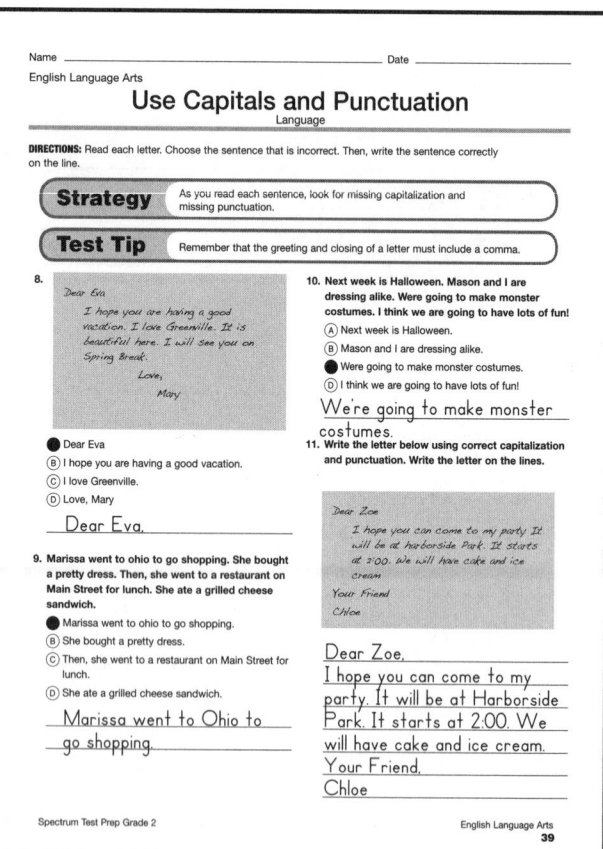

Spectrum Test Prep Grade 2

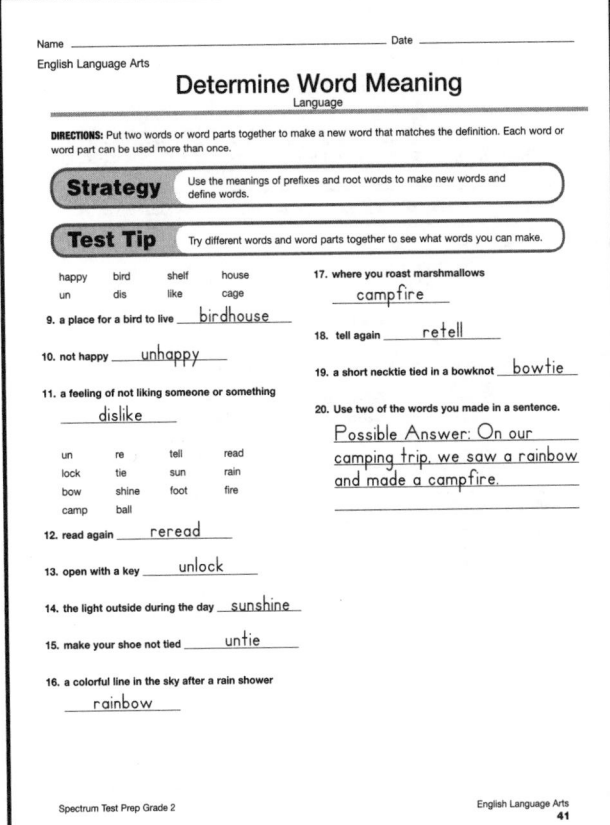

Page 40

Determine Word Meanings
Language

DIRECTIONS: Read each short paragraph. Choose or write the best word to answer each question.

Strategy Use context clues, prefixes, root words, and smaller word parts to help you choose the meaning of words.

Test Tip When choosing the best answer, try each answer choice in the blank.

The _____ was easy to enter. All you had to do was go to the park. To win, you had to _____ how many jelly beans were in the jar.

1. What word should go in the first blank?
   - (A) door
   - ● contest
   - (C) tunnel
   - (D) house

2. What word should go in the second blank?
   - ● guess
   - (B) read
   - (C) count
   - (D) sing

Each house on the block had a _____ backyard. Each had small patches of lawn and flowers. Some even had _____ gardens.

3. What word should go in the first blank?
   - (A) unlikely
   - ● neat
   - (C) lost
   - (D) firm

4. What word should go in the second blank?
   - (A) sand
   - (B) problem
   - ● vegetable
   - (D) blanket

Test Tip
If you know that *un-* means "not," you can find the meaning of the word *unhappy*.

5. Mia was very unhappy because her dog was sick. What does *unhappy* mean?
   - (A) not angry
   - (B) happy again
   - ● not happy
   - (D) excited again

6. Write the meaning of *retell* on the line.
   Please retell your story to the class.

   tell again

Test Tip
Two words that make one new word are compound words. Make sure each part is a word on its own.

7. Write the two words that make up the compound word lighthouse.

   light; house

8. What word has the same root as *bicycle*?
   - (A) biweekly
   - ● recycle
   - (C) binoculars
   - (D) billion

Page 41

Determine Word Meaning
Language

DIRECTIONS: Put two words or word parts together to make a new word that matches the definition. Each word or word part can be used more than once.

Strategy Use the meanings of prefixes and root words to make new words and define words.

Test Tip Try different words and word parts together to see what words you can make.

happy	bird	shelf	house
un	dis	like	cage

9. a place for a bird to live   birdhouse

10. not happy   unhappy

11. a feeling of not liking someone or something
    dislike

un	re	tell	read
lock	tie	sun	rain
bow	shine	foot	fire
camp	ball		

12. read again   reread

13. open with a key   unlock

14. the light outside during the day   sunshine

15. make your shoe not tied   untie

16. a colorful line in the sky after a rain shower
    rainbow

17. where you roast marshmallows
    campfire

18. tell again   retell

19. a short necktie tied in a bowknot   bowtie

20. Use two of the words you made in a sentence.
    Possible Answer: On our camping trip, we saw a rainbow and made a campfire.

Page 42

Determine Shades of Meaning
Language

DIRECTIONS: Order the words in the chart according to their strength.

Strategy Compare words that have similar meanings by asking which word has a stronger meaning. Then, choose the word that fits in the sentence.

Test Tip Some words may seem similar, but they really have different meanings. For example, *hold* and *grab* mean about the same thing. But *hold* makes you think of gently holding something. *Grab* makes you think of holding on tightly.

EXAMPLE

Not Strong	A Little Strong	Strong
big	large	gigantic
jog	run	dash

1.
thin	good	okay	call
skinny	happy	warm	crabby
furious	yell	hurl	scrawny
excellent	toss	hot	angry
thrilled	boiling	cool	shout
cold	throw	pleased	freezing

Not Strong	A Little Strong	Strong
thin	skinny	scrawny
toss	throw	hurl
okay	good	excellent
warm	hot	boiling
cool	cold	freezing
crabby	angry	furious
call	yell	shout
pleased	happy	thrilled

2. Choose the sentences with the underlined word that uses the correct strength of meaning. Choose all that apply.
   - ● The tiny kitten was so skinny he fit in my hand.
   - (B) The snowy, icy day was cool, so I wore a scarf and hat.
   - ● Dan yelled loudly to the woman who hit his car.
   - (D) She was thrilled when she found a penny on the road.

3. What happens if a sentence uses a word that has too strong of a meaning?
   Possible Answer: The word doesn't make sense in the sentence. If the word is too strong, it doesn't go with the rest of the words in the sentence.

Page 43

Determine Shades of Meaning
Language

DIRECTIONS: Read each sentence. Write the word that best fits on the line.

Strategy Use other words in the sentence to help you choose the word with the best meaning.

1. The air was   cool   , so I put on a long-sleeved shirt.
   cool   cold   freezing

2. Be careful! The water on the stove is
    boiling   !
   warm   hot   boiling

Test Tip
While you read, picture the word in your mind to see how strong the word is. Choose the word that matches the meaning of the sentence.

3. I was late for school, so I   sprinted   as fast as I could.
   jogged   ran   sprinted

4. The temperature is -20°F. It is   freezing   outside.
   cool   cold   freezing

5. I   glanced   quickly in the mirror as I dashed out the door.
   glanced   looked   stared

DIRECTIONS: Read each sentence. Rewrite the sentence by replacing the underlined word or words with a word that is stronger.

6. Ella is angry today.
   Possible Answer: Ella is furious today.

7. I don't like Brussels sprouts, but I will eat them if it means getting dessert!
   Possible Answer: I hate Brussels sprouts, but I will eat them if it means getting dessert!

8. We got wet on the boat ride at the amusement park!
   We got soaked on the boat ride at the amusement park!

9. I could see steam from the warm cup of tea.
   I could see steam from the boiling cup of tea.

10. She was pleased to win first prize in the contest!
    She was thrilled to win first prize in the contest!

Page 44

Write an Opinion
Writing

Strategy Plan your writing by stating your opinion and listing reasons you have that opinion. Then, begin writing. When you are finished writing, read your paragraph to yourself. Make sure you included everything listed in the directions. Make sure your writing is clear and fix any errors.

DIRECTIONS: An opinion paragraph tells how you feel about a topic. It gives reasons why you feel that way. Write an opinion paragraph about your favorite place in your town.

Your paragraph should have:
- A sentence to introduce your topic
- A statement of your opinion
- Some reasons for your opinion
- Linking words to connect your opinion and reasons
- A sentence to end your paragraph

Read the example paragraph to see how one student wrote an opinion paragraph about his favorite food.

EXAMPLE
My favorite food is tacos. I like tacos because they are crunchy and spicy. I like to eat my tacos with sour cream and hot sauce. My favorite part of eating tacos is tasting the spicy, delicious meat with the cool, crisp toppings. I think tacos are the best food.

Test Tip A good way to check spelling and punctuation is to read your paragraph backward, from the end to the beginning.

Answer: Student should:
introduce the topic
state an opinion
supply several reasons for the opinion
use linking words
provide a sense of closure

44

Page 45

Write an Opinion
Writing

DIRECTIONS: An opinion paragraph tells how you feel about a topic. It gives reasons why you feel that way. Write an opinion paragraph about your favorite animal.

Your paragraph should have:
- A sentence to introduce your topic
- A statement of your opinion
- Some reasons for your opinion
- Linking words to connect your opinion and reasons
- A sentence to end your paragraph

Read the example paragraph to see how one student wrote an opinion paragraph about her favorite book.

EXAMPLE
My favorite book is *Island of the Blue Dolphins*. I like this book because the main character is a very strong girl. The book is interesting because Karana gets stranded on an island. She is very brave and survives for many years by herself. My favorite thing about this book is that it is based on a true story. I think that *Island of the Blue Dolphins* is a wonderful book.

Answer: Student should:
introduce the topic
state an opinion
supply several reasons for the opinion
use linking words
provide a sense of closure

45

Page 47

Write an Informative Paragraph
Writing

DIRECTIONS: Write your informative paragraph. When you finish, use the checklist below.

Checklist:
- [ ] I have a clear topic sentence.
- [ ] I have details that support my topic.
- [ ] I used nouns correctly.
- [ ] I used pronouns correctly.
- [ ] I used verbs correctly.
- [ ] I used adjectives and adverbs to make my writing interesting.

Answer: Student should:
introduce the topic
state several facts that support the topic
include definitions
provide a sense of closure
use nouns and pronouns correctly
use verbs (esp. irregular past tense) correctly
use adjectives and adverbs

47

Page 49

Write an Explanatory Paragraph
Writing

DIRECTIONS: Write your explanatory paragraph. When you finish, use the checklist below.

Test Tip Use words like *first*, *next*, *then*, and *finally* to show the order of steps to follow.

Checklist:
- [ ] I have a clear topic sentence.
- [ ] I have clear steps to follow.
- [ ] I have facts and definitions that support my topic.
- [ ] I used nouns correctly.
- [ ] I used pronouns correctly.
- [ ] I used verbs correctly.
- [ ] I used adjectives and adverbs to make my writing interesting.

Answer: Student should:
introduce the topic
state several facts that support the topic
include definitions
provide a sense of closure
use nouns and pronouns correctly
use verbs (esp. irregular past tense) correctly
use adjectives and adverbs

49

Page 51

Write a Narrative
Writing

DIRECTIONS: Write your narrative. When you finish, use the checklist below.

Test Tip — Use the checklist below to make sure you have everything in your paragraph.

Checklist
- ☐ I wrote about an event that happened in my life.
- ☐ I have clear details that tell about the event.
- ☐ I included details about my thoughts, feelings, and actions.
- ☐ I used pronouns correctly.
- ☐ I have a satisfying ending.

Answer: Student should:
Recount two or more sequenced events
Include details of what happened
Include thoughts, feelings, and actions
Use temporal words
Provide a sense of closure
Use reflexive pronouns correctly

Page 52

Strategy Review

In this section, you will review the strategies you learned and apply them to practice the skills.

Strategy — Use details from a story or passage to show your understanding.

It was a rainy afternoon. Ty sat in his house watching the rain slide down the front window. His sister was taking a nap. His mom was cleaning the kitchen. Ty didn't know what to do. There was nothing on TV. The computer was broken. He got up and wandered to the basement. There were boxes and stacks of paper, old books, and photo albums. Ty wandered and peeked in boxes. An hour later, his mom called him. He ran upstairs.
"What have you been doing in that dirty basement?" his mom asked.
Ty pulled on his mom's hand. "Come and see, Mom," he said. They went down the stairs. Ty led his mom through the maze of old junk. Finally, he stopped. His mom looked at the giant cardboard robot in front of her.
"Oh, my!" she said. "You have been very busy."

First, read the story. Think about what a rainy day is like.
Next, make a connection. What do you like to do on rainy days?
Finally, read the questions that go with the story. Think about what you read or look back at the story. You can pick out key words in the question and look for those words in the story to find the answer quickly.

1. Why was Ty looking for something to do?
- Ⓐ He was home sick from school.
- Ⓑ It was snowing and he couldn't go outside.
- Ⓒ The TV was broken.
- ● It was raining and he had nothing to do.

2. How did Ty solve his problem?
Possible Answer: He built a robot out of old boxes.

Read the next story about a rainy day. Think about how it is the same as the story you just read. Think about how it is different.

Jess was home alone. Mom and Dad were at work. She didn't usually mind being alone, but today she was bored.
"There's nothing to do!" she complained to her dog, Sally.
Sally looked at Jess, but said nothing.
"You're no help," Jess said, patting the beagle's brown head.

Jess flipped on the TV. Nothing. She picked up a book and started reading. She just couldn't get into the story. Finally, Jess went upstairs to her bedroom.
Jess looked around her room for something to do. Suddenly, she spotted the new art set her aunt had bought her for her last birthday.
"Well," thought Jess, "it's something to do."
Jess opened the art set and began creating. When her mom called at lunchtime, Jess ran to the phone.
"I'm fine, Mom," she answered. "But, I can't talk right now. I'm really busy."

3. Why was Jess looking for something to do?
Possible Answer: She was home alone and bored.

4. Write how the two stories are alike.
Possible Answer: Both stories are about children using their imaginations to entertain themselves when they are bored.

Page 53

Strategy Review

Strategy — While reading, look carefully at pictures to help you better understand the story or passage.

When you read stories or informational text, there are often pictures, too. The pictures are there to help you understand the words better. An author carefully chooses pictures that will support the main idea of the story or passage.

Read the passage and look at the picture. Then, answer the questions.

Changing Phones
Technology changes quickly. One form of technology that has changed a lot since it was first invented is the telephone. When Alexander Graham Bell invented the first telephone in 1876, he shaped it like a metal cone. It had a thin piece of paper stretched like a drum over one end. A cork with a needle stuck in it was glued to the outside of the paper.
Phones have changed greatly from that first model. For decades, most people have had at least one phone in their home. The first phones had a separate earpiece and mouthpiece. Then, the two were combined into one. Early home phones were hard-wired into the home. You could not talk on the phone if you weren't connected to the wall! Later, cordless phones were invented. Finally, you could call your friend and wander throughout the house chatting. But, you still could not go very far away from the phone's base.
The first mobile phone was invented in 1973. The handset weighed 2.2 pounds! The cell phones most people have today have evolved from that first mobile phone. Who knows what the future will bring?

First, read the passage and make connections to the details. How are the phones mentioned in the story alike? How are they different?
Next, study the picture. Ask yourself how the picture adds details that are not in the passage.
Finally, read the questions that go with the passage. Use the picture and details from the passage to help you answer the questions.

1. Write what one model of the telephone looked like.
Possible Answer: It was bulky and had a cord connecting the handset to the phone.

2. Choose two ways the phone in the picture is different from the first phone.
- Ⓐ The first phone was shaped like a donut.
- ● The first phone was shaped like a cone.
- ● The first phone did not have a handset.
- Ⓓ The first phone could be used anywhere.

How did the strategy help you answer these questions?
Possible answer: The picture gave details about the telephone that the passage did not.

Page 54

Strategy Review

STRATEGIES
- Look for connecting words like *because* and *so* to understand why something happens in a passage.
- Look for words that explain the meaning of new words. Looking for commas or the keyword can help you find these words.
- Plan your writing.
- When you write, use details to support main ideas.

EXAMPLE
Sabrina likes to go spelunking, or exploring caves, on weekends.
What is spelunking?
First, look for the new word.
Sabrina likes to go spelunking, or exploring caves, on weekends.
Next, look for the keyword or and commas.
Sabrina likes to go spelunking, or exploring caves, on weekends.
Spelunking means exploring caves.

Choose the part of the sentence that answers the question.

1. Adam is using crutches because he sprained his ankle in a soccer game. Why is Adam using crutches?
- Ⓐ Adam is
- Ⓑ using crutches
- ● because he sprained his ankle
- Ⓓ in a soccer game

2. Abe likes to eat latkes, fried potato pancakes, when he goes to his aunt's house for Passover. What are latkes?
- Ⓐ Abe likes to eat latkes
- ● fried potato pancakes
- Ⓒ when he goes to his aunt's house
- Ⓓ for Passover

Example
Write a paragraph that tells how to brush your teeth.
Start by planning your paragraph.
First, list the steps you must follow.
1. get toothbrush and toothpaste
2. put toothpaste on the toothbrush
3. rub the toothpaste into your teeth for 2 minutes
4. rinse the toothpaste out of your mouth
5. clean off your toothbrush

Then, add details and write your paragraph.
There are important steps to brushing your teeth. First, you will need a toothbrush and toothpaste. Squeeze toothpaste onto the toothbrush. Then, rub the toothpaste into your teeth. Brush all of your teeth on all sides. Do this for two minutes. Next, rinse the toothpaste out of your mouth with water. Finally, clean your toothbrush so it is ready for next time.

3. Write a paragraph about how to eat a bowl of cereal. First, plan your paragraph by writing the steps of eating cereal. Possible Answers:
1. Pour cereal into a bowl.
2. Add milk to the cereal.
3. Use a spoon to eat the cereal.

4. Add details and write your paragraph on the lines.
Student should write a paragraph that clearly describes how to eat a bowl of cereal.

Page 55

Strategy Review

Write a story about getting ready for school.

This morning I got up early for school. First, I took a shower and brushed my teeth. Next, I dressed in nice, warm clothes. After that, I dried and combed my hair. I ate breakfast and then had to brush my teeth again! Finally, I put on my coat and hat, grabbed my backpack, and headed to the bus stop.

1. Write a short story about visiting a zoo, park, or museum. First, plan your paragraph by writing the events in order from first to last.

Students should include a list of events that happened on the visit.

2. Add details and write your paragraph on the lines.

Students should write a story using events that occur in order from beginning to end.

Strategy — Revise to make sure your writing makes sense. Then, edit to fix errors.

After you write your first draft, you should read it over. Read the story out loud to yourself to make sure it makes sense. Look for places where the reader might have trouble understanding what you wanted to say. Look for words that need capitals. Look for places that need punctuation marks. Finally, look for words that might be spelled wrong.

Spectrum Test Prep Grade 2

English Language Arts
55

Page 57

Solve One-Step Problems: Add and Subtract
Numbers and Operations

DIRECTIONS: Choose the best answer.

EXAMPLE

30 cows are in the field. 15 cows are in the barn. Write a number sentence that you can use to find how many cows there are in all. Use a ☐ for the number of cows in all.

☐ _____ ☐ = ☐

Answer: 30 + 15 = ☐

Solve your number sentence and tell how many cows there are in all.

30 + 15 = ☐

Answer: 30 + 15 = 45; There are 45 cows in all.

Strategy — Use drawings, number sentences, and basic facts to solve word problems.

Test Tip — First, think about what question is being asked in the problem. Then, decide if you need to add or subtract.

1. There are 49 ants in Lila's ant farm. Lila bought more ants to put in the ant farm. There are now 67 ants in her ant farm. Write a number sentence that you can use to find how many ants Lila bought. The ☐ stands for the number of ants Lila bought.

_67_ - _49_ = ☐

How did you find your answer?

Subtract 49 from 67 to find out how many ants Lila bought (18 ants).

Test Tip — Words like *how much farther, how many were left,* and *how much more* usually mean you will need to subtract.

2. Cheri and Katrina were having a baseball throwing contest. Cheri threw the baseball 56 feet. Katrina threw the ball 68 feet. How much farther did Katrina throw the ball than Cheri? Explain how you found your answer.

Katrina threw the ball 12 feet farther. Subtract 56 from 68 to find how much farther: 68 - 56 = 12.

3. Kia had some math problems to do for homework. She did 5 problems. There were 10 problems still left to do. Which number sentences show this situation? Choose all that apply.

● A. 15 − 5 = 10
○ B. 10 − 5 = 5
○ C. 15 + 5 = 20
● D. 5 + 10 = 15

Spectrum Test Prep Grade 2

Math
57

Page 58

Solve One-Step Problems: Add and Subtract
Numbers and Operations

DIRECTIONS: Choose the best answer.

Strategy — Draw the number of objects in a word problem and find clue words that tell if you are adding or subtracting. Then, use the picture and clue words to write a number sentence.

Test Tip — Words like *in all, all together,* and *total* usually mean you will need to add.

4. Lisa practiced the violin for 35 minutes on Monday and 46 minutes on Wednesday. Which number sentence shows how many minutes in all Lisa practiced on Monday and Wednesday?

● A. 35 + 46 = 81
○ B. 46 − 35 = 11
○ C. 11 + 35 = 66
○ D. 81 + 35 = 116

5. Dara's grandmother is 48 years old. Her grandfather is 51 years old. Which number sentence shows how much older Dara's grandfather is than Dara's grandmother?

○ A. 48 + 51 = 99
● B. 51 − 48 = 3
○ C. 48 + 3 = 51
○ D. 99 − 51 = 48

Write how you know.

Possible Answer: I subtract 51 and 48 to get how much older Dara's grandfather is.

6. Felipe has 17 nickels in his coin bank. His dad gave him 8 more nickels to put in his bank. How many nickels does Felipe have in his coin bank now? Draw a picture and write a number sentence to show how you found your answer.

Possible answers: a picture of 17 circles (coins) plus 8 more for a total of 25 circles; 17 + 8 = 25

7. Sandra wants to make a quilt using a total of 19 green and yellow squares of cloth. She can use any number of green and yellow squares as long as they total 19. How many yellow squares and how many green squares could Sandra use to make her quilt? Use words, numbers, or pictures to show how you found your answer.

Possible answers: a picture of 10 plain squares plus 9 shaded squares to show 19 all together; words: I add 10 squares to 9 squares to total 19; number sentence such as 10 + 9 = 19. 12 + 7 = 19. or 13 + 6 = 19

8. Mandy's uncle has 12 horses on his farm. He has 17 more cows than horses. Write a number sentence that shows how many cows Mandy's uncle has.

Possible Answer: 17 + 12 = ☐

Now, solve the problem.

Answer: 17 + 12 = 29

Math
58

Spectrum Test Prep Grade 2

Page 59

Solve Two-Step Problems: Add and Subtract
Numbers and Operations

DIRECTIONS: Choose or write the correct answer.

Strategy — Use clue words and basic addition and subtraction facts to solve problems. First, think about what question is being asked in the problem. Then, decide if you need to add or subtract, or do both operations.

Test Tip — A number sentence includes symbols such as +, −, and =.

EXAMPLE

Luisa picked some berries. She put 50 strawberries in a basket. Then, she ate 15 of the berries before picking 11 more. Write a number sentence that you can use to find how many berries are left in the basket. Use a ☐ for the number of berries left.

Answer: 50 − 15 + 11 = ☐

Solve your number sentence.

Answer: 50 − 15 + 11 = 46

1. Jeff and his family are going to his uncle's house. They drive 45 minutes. Jeff's dad spends another 12 minutes getting gas and 5 minutes waiting in traffic. How long does it take the family to make the trip? Write a number sentence that you can use to find how long the trip takes. Use a ☐ for the unknown number.

_45 + 12 + 5 = ☐_

Solve your number sentence and tell how long it takes the family to make the trip.

45 + 12 + 5 = 62; The trip takes 62 minutes.

2. At the county fair, Jamal wants to go on 8 rides and play 5 games. When he gets there, he decides not to go on 2 of the rides. How many activities did Jamal do all together at the county fair? Show how you got your answer.

_11; 8 + 5 − 2 = 11; or 8 + 5 = 13, 13 − 2 = 11_

3. Leesa has 20 math problems for homework. She does 5 problems after school and 4 more problems after piano practice. How many problems does Leesa have left to do? Which number sentence shows this situation? Choose all that apply.

● A. 20 − 5 − 4 = 11
○ B. 20 − 5 + 4 = 19
○ C. 20 − 5 − 4 = 11
○ D. 20 − 5 + 4 = 19

4. Tomas has 10 balls and 3 bats. He gives Kiley 4 balls. Then, he gives Carlo 1 bat. Which number sentence can you use to find how many balls and bats in all Tomas has left? Choose all that apply.

● A. 10 + 3 − 4 − 1 = ☐
○ B. 13 − 4 − 1 = ☐
● C. 10 + 3 − 5 = ☐
○ D. 10 − 3 + 5 − 4 = ☐

5. Angela wrote this number sentence to solve a problem.

10 − 8 + ☐ = 9

Write a word problem that Angela might have solved.

Possible Answer: Mrs. Casey baked 10 muffins. Sean and his friends ate 8 muffins. Then, Mrs. Casey baked some more muffins. There are now 9 muffins. How many more muffins did Mrs. Casey bake?

Spectrum Test Prep Grade 2

Math
59

Page 76

Name _____ Date _____
Math

Add and Subtract Within 100
Number and Operations

Strategy Write number sentences for word problems to help you understand what is being added or subtracted.

6. Janie bought some mustard at the store. The mustard cost 67 cents. She bought some yogurt that cost 28 cents more than the mustard. How much did the yogurt cost? Choose the best answer.

Ⓐ 39 cents
Ⓑ 85 cents
Ⓒ 91 cents
● 95 cents

Write how you know.

Possible Answer: I write the number sentence 67 + 28 = ☐. Then I add the ones, 7 + 8 = 15 and the tens, 60 + 20 = 80. 15 + 80 = 95.

7. Jason drew 36 circles on a piece of paper. He colored 15 of them red and 12 of them green. How many circles are other colors? Use words, numbers, or pictures.

36 – 15 – 12 = 9; 9 are other colors; a picture of 36 circles, with 15 + 12 or 27 of them shaded to show 9 unshaded

8. Two girls solved the same problem different ways. Choose one way and explain why it is correct.

Laura's Way	Lindsay's Way
35 + 25	35 + 25
30 + 20 + 5 +5	25 + 25 + 10

35 + 25 = 60; Lauren's Way: 30 + 20 = 50; 5 + 5 = 10; so, 50 + 10 = 60; Lindsay's Way: 25 + 25 = 50 and 10 more added on is 60.

DIRECTIONS: Write a number in the ☐ to make the number sentence true for questions 9 and 10.

9. 63 + 14 = ☐14☐ + 63

10. 64 – 10 + 26 = 64 + ☐26☐ –10

11. Yuri tried to pick up a box of 51 books. It was too heavy, so he took out 19 books. How many books are now in the box? Solve the problem and show your work. Use words, numbers, or pictures.

51 – 19 = 32; or using place value, break 51 into 40 + 10 + 1 and 19 into 10 + 9; subtract 40 – 10 = 30 and 11 – 9 = 2; 30 + 2 = 32

Math
76

Spectrum Test Prep Grade 2

76

Page 77

Name _____ Date _____
Math

Add and Subtract Within 1,000
Number and Operations

DIRECTIONS: Answer the questions.

Strategy To add and subtract three-digit numbers, use place value: add or subtract the hundreds, then, add or subtract the tens, then, add or subtract the ones.

EXAMPLE

The music store had 457 customers last month and 262 customers this month. How many customers did the store have all together in those two months? Choose the best answer.

Ⓐ 195
Ⓑ 619
Ⓒ 709
Ⓓ 719

Answer: D

Test Tip

You might find it helpful to use scratch paper to draw pictures or record information to solve a problem.

1. Cody played 3 video games. In the first game, he scored 117 points. In the second game, he scored 222 points. In the third game, he scored 60 points less points than in his first game. How many points did he score all together?

Ⓐ 339
● 396
Ⓒ 399
Ⓓ 401

Write how you know.
Possible Answer: I write a number sentence to add the points of the first and second game: 117 + 222 = ☐ I solve the problem: 7 and 2 ones make 9 ones; 1 and 2 tens make 30 tens; 1 hundred and 2 hundreds

make 3 hundreds. 117 + 222 = 339. Then I write a number sentence to find the score of the third game: 117 - 60 = ☐. 7 ones less 0 ones is 7. 1 ten less 6 tens is 50, regrouping or borrowing from the hundreds. So the third game has 57 points. So Cody scored 339 + 57 = 396.

2. Nicole used blocks to solve a problem. Write a number sentence that shows the problem Nicole solved.

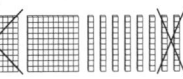

280 – 120 = 160

3. One plane has 211 people. Another plane has 328 people. Write in the place-value chart to show how to find the total number of people on the two planes.

	Hundreds	Tens	Ones
Plane 1:	2	1	1
Plane 2:	3	2	8
TOTAL:	5	3	9

Math
77

77

Page 78

Name _____ Date _____
Math

Add and Subtract Within 1,000
Number and Operations

Strategy Draw tables to show hundreds, tens, and ones and compare both three-digit numbers. Or, draw boxes for each place value and compare hundreds, tens, and ones in each number.

Test Tip Read all parts of the question first.

DIRECTIONS: The chart shows the number of students in Grades 1–4 at Hometown School. Use the chart to answer questions 4–6.

Grade	Number of Students
Grade 1	127
Grade 2	134
Grade 3	111
Grade 4	98

4. How many total students are in grades 1–4?

Answer: 470 students

5. Did you need to regroup to find the total? Write why or why not.

Possible Answer: Yes; I regrouped ones and tens. The ones totaled 20 ones, so I regrouped them into 2 tens. I added the 2 tens to 15 tens to make 17 tens. Then, I regrouped 10 tens into 1 hundred.

6. How many more students are in grades 1 and 2 than in grades 3 and 4? Write how you know.

Answer: 52 students; add: 127 + 134 = 261 students in grades 1 and 2; add 111 + 98 = 209 students in grades 3 and 4. Then, subtract 261 – 209 to get 52.

7. Lia has 3 packs of sports cards. Pack 1 has 46 cards and pack 2 has 55 cards. Pack 3 has 5 fewer cards than pack 2. Which number sentences can be used to find how many cards Lia has in all? Choose all that apply.

● 40 + 50 + 50 + 6 + 5 = 151
Ⓑ 40 + 50 + 6 + 5 = 105
● 46 + 55 + 50 = 151
Ⓓ 46 + 55 – 5 = 96

8. For which problems do you need to regroup? Choose all that apply.

● 56 + 39
● 385 – 142
● 912 – 83
Ⓓ 49 + 5

9. The months of September, November, April and June each have 30 days. The blocks below show the number of total days for September, April, and June. Use as few blocks as possible to show the total number of days for September, November, April and June. Draw a picture and write how you know.

Possible Answer: a drawing of 1 hundreds block and 2 tens rods; 30 + 30 + 30 + 30 = 120.

Math
78

Spectrum Test Prep Grade 2

78

Page 79

Name _____ Date _____
Math

Use Mental Math: Add and Subtract 10 and 100
Number and Operations

DIRECTIONS: Choose or write the correct answer.

Strategy Use mental math and place value to add and subtract 10 and 100 to greater numbers. Count up or count back by tens or hundreds.

EXAMPLE

There are black and brown beans in a jar. There are 354 brown beans in the jar. There are 100 less black beans than brown beans. How many black beans are in the jar?
Answer: 100 less than 354 is 254.

1. Cary and Lia are counting their stickers. Cary has 10 more stickers than Lia. Lia has 224 stickers. How many stickers does Cary have?

Ⓐ 214
Ⓑ 324
Ⓒ 124
● 234

Write how you know.
Possible Answer: I count up by tens. In 224, there are 2 tens. Adding or counting up by 1 ten makes 234.

2. Liza said that 100 more than 562 is 572. What did Liza do wrong?

Possible Answer: Liza added 10 instead of 100. 100 more than 562 is 662.

3. Mrs. Como read a book with 478 pages. Mr. Como read a book with 100 less pages. How many pages are in Mr. Como's book?

● 378
Ⓑ 488
Ⓒ 468
Ⓓ 278

Test Tip

To quickly add 10 to a number, increase the tens digit by 1. To add 100 to a number, increase the hundreds digit by 1.

DIRECTIONS: Write 10 less and 10 more than the given number for questions 4–7.

4. 643 (10 less) 653 663 (10 more)

5. 145 (10 less) 155 165 (10 more)

6. 274 (10 less) 284 294 (10 more)

7. 701 (10 less) 711 721 (10 more)

DIRECTIONS: Write 100 less and 100 more than the given number for questions 8–11.

8. 403 (100 less) 503 603 (100 more)

9. 77 (100 less) 177 277 (100 more)

10. 189 (100 less) 289 389 (100 more)

11. 791 (100 less) 891 991 (100 more)

Spectrum Test Prep Grade 2

Math
79

79

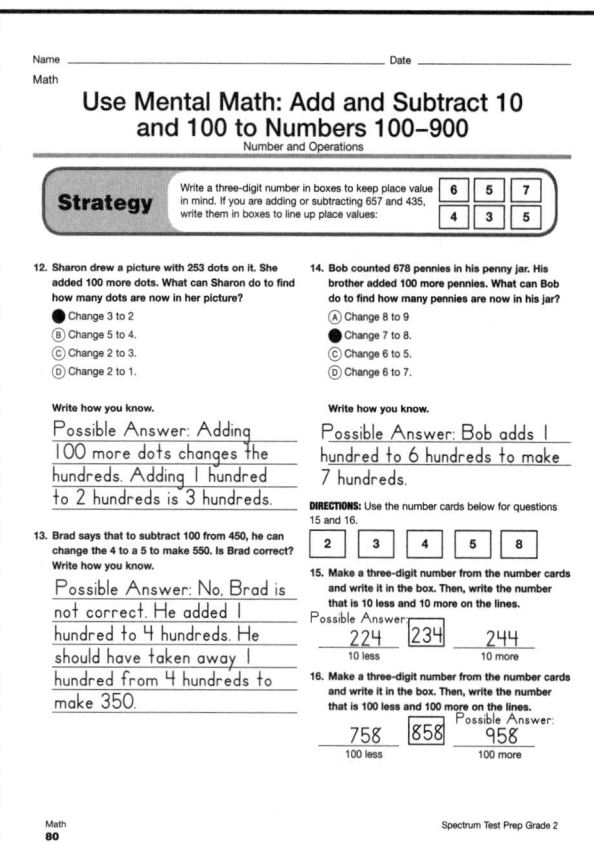

Page 80

Use Mental Math: Add and Subtract 10 and 100 to Numbers 100–900
Number and Operations

Strategy — Write a three-digit number in boxes to keep place value in mind. If you are adding or subtracting 657 and 435, write them in boxes to line up place values:

6	5	7
4	3	5

12. Sharon drew a picture with 253 dots on it. She added 100 more dots. What can Sharon do to find how many dots are now in her picture?
● A Change 3 to 2
B Change 5 to 4.
C Change 2 to 3.
D Change 2 to 1.

Write how you know.

Possible Answer: Adding 100 more dots changes the hundreds. Adding 1 hundred to 2 hundreds is 3 hundreds.

13. Brad says that to subtract 100 from 450, he can change the 4 to a 5 to make 550. Is Brad correct? Write how you know.

Possible Answer: No, Brad is not correct. He added 1 hundred to 4 hundreds. He should have taken away 1 hundred from 4 hundreds to make 350.

14. Bob counted 678 pennies in his penny jar. His brother added 100 more pennies. What can Bob do to find how many pennies are now in his jar?
A Change 8 to 9
● B Change 7 to 8.
C Change 6 to 5.
D Change 6 to 7.

Write how you know.

Possible Answer: Bob adds 1 hundred to 6 hundreds to make 7 hundreds.

DIRECTIONS: Use the number cards below for questions 15 and 16.

| 2 | 3 | 4 | 5 | 8 |

15. Make a three-digit number from the number cards and write it in the box. Then, write the number that is 10 less and 10 more on the lines.
Possible Answer:
224 (10 less) | 234 | 244 (10 more)

16. Make a three-digit number from the number cards and write it in the box. Then, write the number that is 100 less and 100 more on the lines.
Possible Answer:
758 (100 less) | 858 | 958 (100 more)

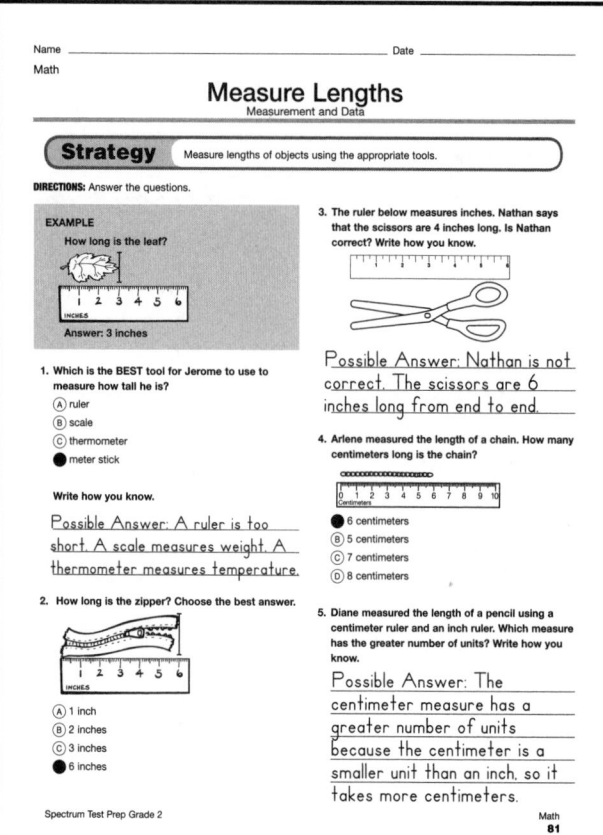

Page 81

Measure Lengths
Measurement and Data

Strategy — Measure lengths of objects using the appropriate tools.

DIRECTIONS: Answer the questions.

EXAMPLE
How long is the leaf?
Answer: 3 inches

1. Which is the BEST tool for Jerome to use to measure how tall he is?
A ruler
B scale
C thermometer
● meter stick

Write how you know.

Possible Answer: A ruler is too short. A scale measures weight. A thermometer measures temperature.

2. How long is the zipper? Choose the best answer.
A 1 inch
B 2 inches
C 3 inches
● 6 inches

3. The ruler below measures inches. Nathan says that the scissors are 4 inches long. Is Nathan correct? Write how you know.

Possible Answer: Nathan is not correct. The scissors are 6 inches long from end to end.

4. Arlene measured the length of a chain. How many centimeters long is the chain?
● 6 centimeters
B 5 centimeters
C 7 centimeters
D 8 centimeters

5. Diane measured the length of a pencil using a centimeter ruler and an inch ruler. Which measure has the greater number of units? Write how you know.

Possible Answer: The centimeter measure has a greater number of units because the centimeter is a smaller unit than an inch, so it takes more centimeters.

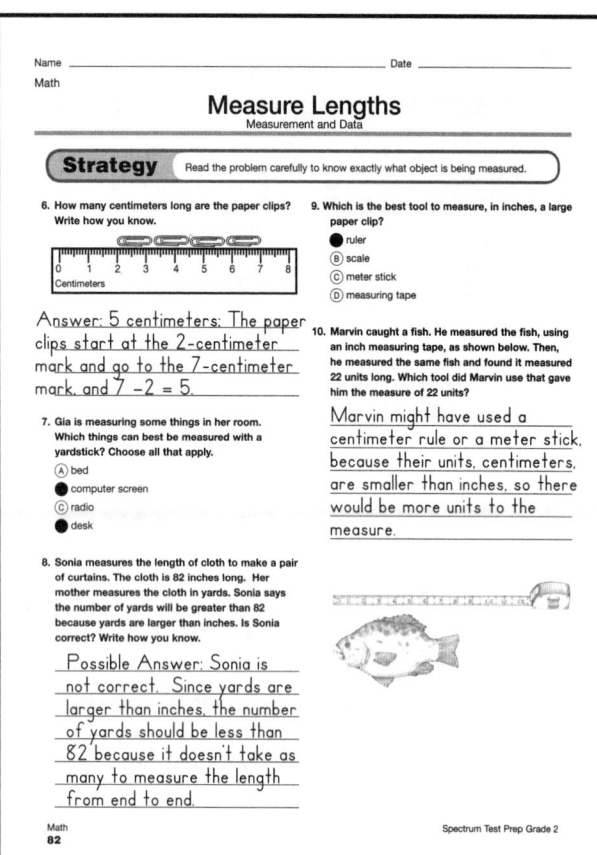

Page 82

Measure Lengths
Measurement and Data

Strategy — Read the problem carefully to know exactly what object is being measured.

6. How many centimeters long are the paper clips? Write how you know.

Answer: 5 centimeters; The paper clips start at the 2-centimeter mark and go to the 7-centimeter mark, and 7 − 2 = 5.

7. Gia is measuring some things in her room. Which things can best be measured with a yardstick? Choose all that apply.
A bed
● computer screen
C radio
● desk

8. Sonia measures the length of cloth to make a pair of curtains. The cloth is 82 inches long. Her mother measures the cloth in yards. Sonia says the number of yards will be greater than 82 because yards are larger than inches. Is Sonia correct? Write how you know.

Possible Answer: Sonia is not correct. Since yards are larger than inches, the number of yards should be less than 82 because it doesn't take as many to measure the length from end to end.

9. Which is the best tool to measure, in inches, a large paper clip?
● ruler
B scale
C meter stick
D measuring tape

10. Marvin caught a fish. He measured the fish, using an inch measuring tape, as shown below. Then, he measured the same fish and found it measured 22 units long. Which tool did Marvin use that gave him the measure of 22 units?

Marvin might have used a centimeter rule or a meter stick, because their units, centimeters, are smaller than inches, so there would be more units to the measure.

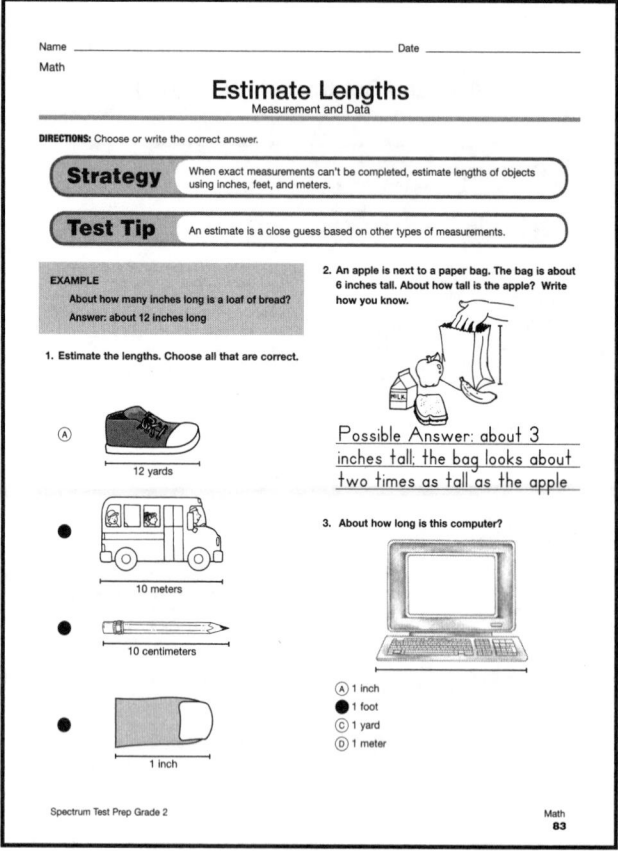

Page 83

Estimate Lengths
Measurement and Data

DIRECTIONS: Choose or write the correct answer.

Strategy — When exact measurements can't be completed, estimate lengths of objects using inches, feet, and meters.

Test Tip — An estimate is a close guess based on other types of measurements.

EXAMPLE
About how many inches long is a loaf of bread?
Answer: about 12 inches long

1. Estimate the lengths. Choose all that are correct.
A — 12 yards
● — 10 meters
● — 10 centimeters
● — 1 inch

2. An apple is next to a paper bag. The bag is about 6 inches tall. About how tall is the apple? Write how you know.

Possible Answer: about 3 inches tall; the bag looks about two times as tall as the apple

3. About how long is this computer?
A 1 inch
● 1 foot
C 1 yard
D 1 meter

Estimate Lengths
Measurement and Data

Strategy — When estimating, compare two objects. Are they about the same size? Is one object half the size of the other object?

4. Mr. Jackson is about 6 feet tall. He is standing next to his young son. About how tall is his son? Write how you know.

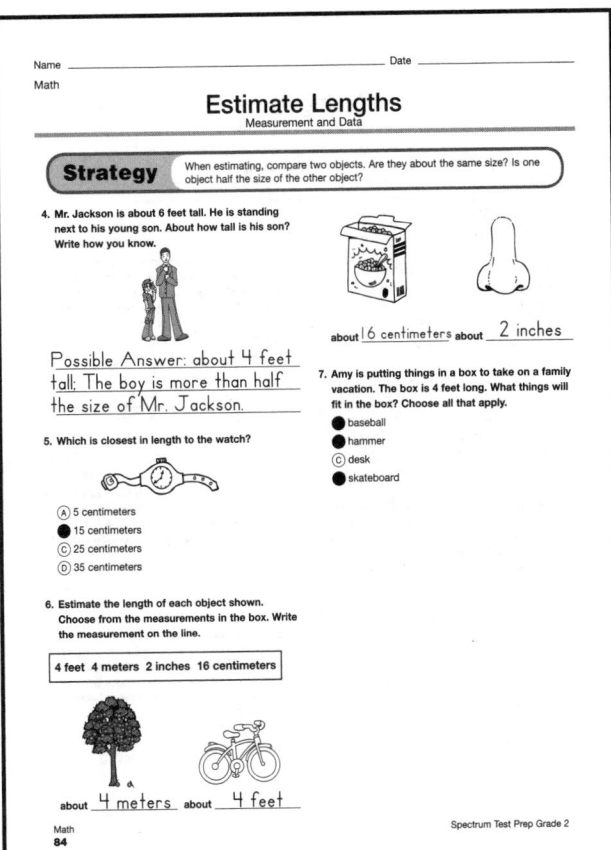

about 16 centimeters   about 2 inches

Possible Answer: about 4 feet tall; The boy is more than half the size of Mr. Jackson.

5. Which is closest in length to the watch?

Ⓐ 5 centimeters
● 15 centimeters
Ⓒ 25 centimeters
Ⓓ 35 centimeters

7. Amy is putting things in a box to take on a family vacation. The box is 4 feet long. What things will fit in the box? Choose all that apply.

● baseball
● hammer
Ⓒ desk
● skateboard

6. Estimate the length of each object shown. Choose from the measurements in the box. Write the measurement on the line.

| 4 feet 4 meters 2 inches 16 centimeters |

about 4 meters   about 4 feet

84

Find Difference in Lengths
Measurement and Data

DIRECTIONS: Answer the questions.

Strategy — Use adding and subtracting strategies to find the differences in lengths of objects. Find the sum by adding lengths and find the difference by subtracting lengths.

EXAMPLE

Use an inch ruler to measure the arrows. How many inches longer is arrow B than arrow A?

A   B

Answer: 2 inches

1. Look at the leaf below. How many inches long must another leaf be to measure 3 inches longer than this leaf?

● 6 inches
Ⓑ 4 inches
Ⓒ 3 inches
Ⓓ 2 inches

2. Look at the leaf in question 1. What is the difference in length between the leaf and the zipper?

● 3 inches
Ⓑ 5 inches
Ⓒ 6 inches
Ⓓ 9 inches

3. Use your centimeter ruler to measure the pencil and the marker. How many centimeters longer is the marker than the pencil? Write how you know.

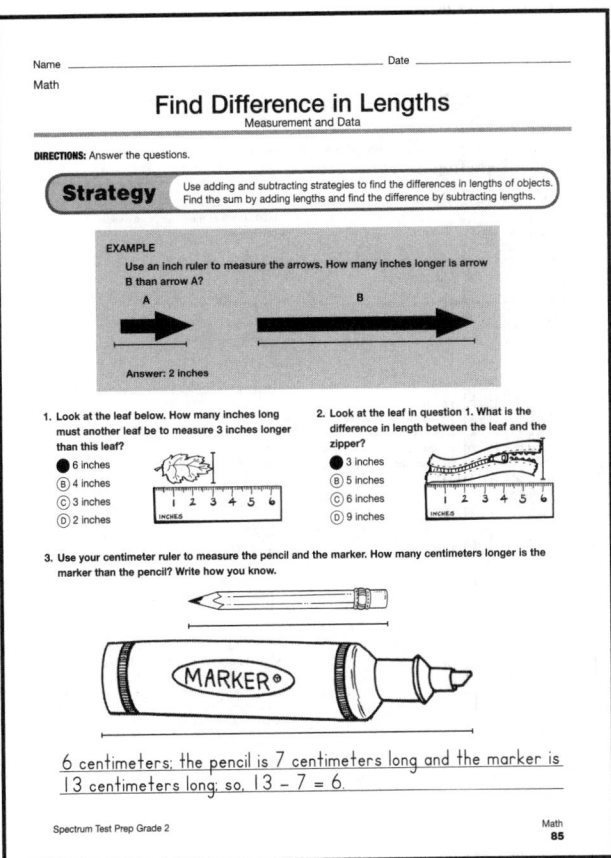

6 centimeters; the pencil is 7 centimeters long and the marker is 13 centimeters long; so, 13 – 7 = 6.

85

Find Difference in Lengths
Measurement and Data

Strategy — Write number sentences to know which measurements to add or subtract and to compare lengths.

DIRECTIONS: Use the pictures of the scissors and box to answer questions 4 and 5.

4. Measure the scissors and the box with a centimeter ruler. Write the measures below each item.

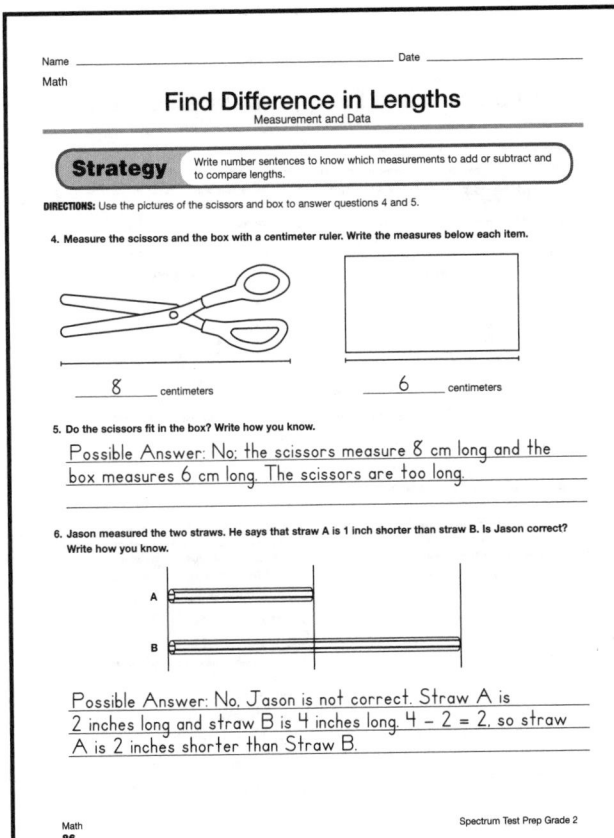

8 centimeters   6 centimeters

5. Do the scissors fit in the box? Write how you know.

Possible Answer: No; the scissors measure 8 cm long and the box measures 6 cm long. The scissors are too long.

6. Jason measured the two straws. He says that straw A is 1 inch shorter than straw B. Is Jason correct? Write how you know.

A

B

Possible Answer: No, Jason is not correct. Straw A is 2 inches long and straw B is 4 inches long. 4 – 2 = 2, so straw A is 2 inches shorter than Straw B.

86

Solve Length Problems: Add and Subtract
Measurement and Data

DIRECTIONS: Answer the questions.

Strategy — Read word problems carefully to identify clue words about adding or subtracting to solve problems about length.

EXAMPLE

Mr. Snell has two pieces of wood. The total length of the two pieces of wood is 35 feet. One piece is 18 feet long. Which is a way to find the length of the second piece of wood? Choose all that apply.

Ⓐ 18 + ☐ = 35
Ⓑ 35 + ☐ = 18
Ⓒ 35 + 18 = ☐
Ⓓ 35 – 18 = ☐

Answer: A, D

Test Tip — Draw a picture to help you answer the problem.

1. At the basketball game, Lee made a basket from 33 feet away. Last year he made a basket from 24 feet away. Write a number sentence to find how much farther away Lee made a basket last year than this year. Then, solve the problem. Use a ? for the unknown number.

33 – 24 = ?; or 24 + ? = 33; ? = 9; Lee made a basket 9 feet farther away this year.

2. Haley made a scarf that is 48 inches long. Luz made a scarf that is 5 inches shorter than Haley's. What is the total length of both scarves? Show how you found the answer.

91 inches; 48 + 48 – 5 = 91

3. Leon measured these two leaves. Then, he found another leaf and measured it. The third leaf is 10 inches long. What is the total length of the 3 leaves?

Ⓐ 3 inches
Ⓑ 6 inches
Ⓒ 13 inches
● 16 inches

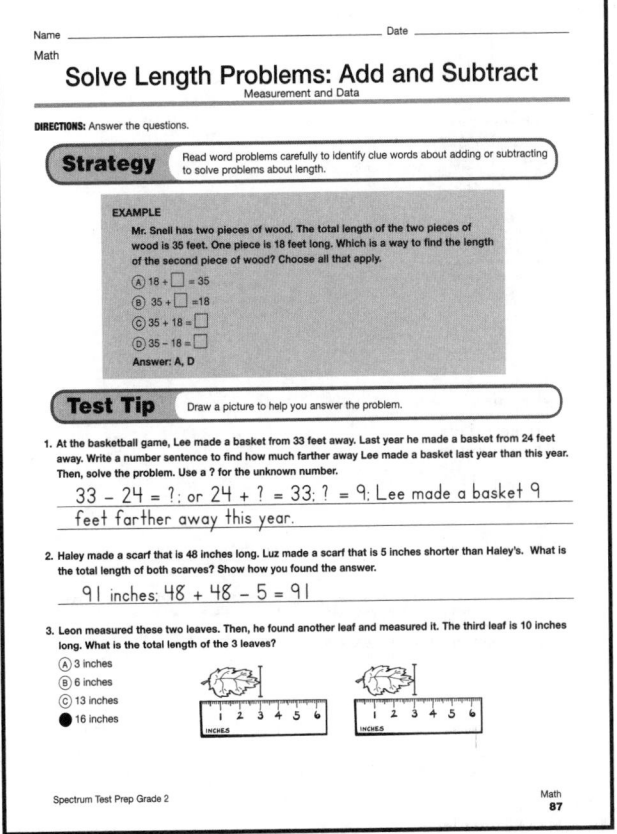

87

Determine Difference in Lengths
Measurement and Data

Strategy Use number sentences to solve problems about length.

1. How much longer is the long straw than the short straw?

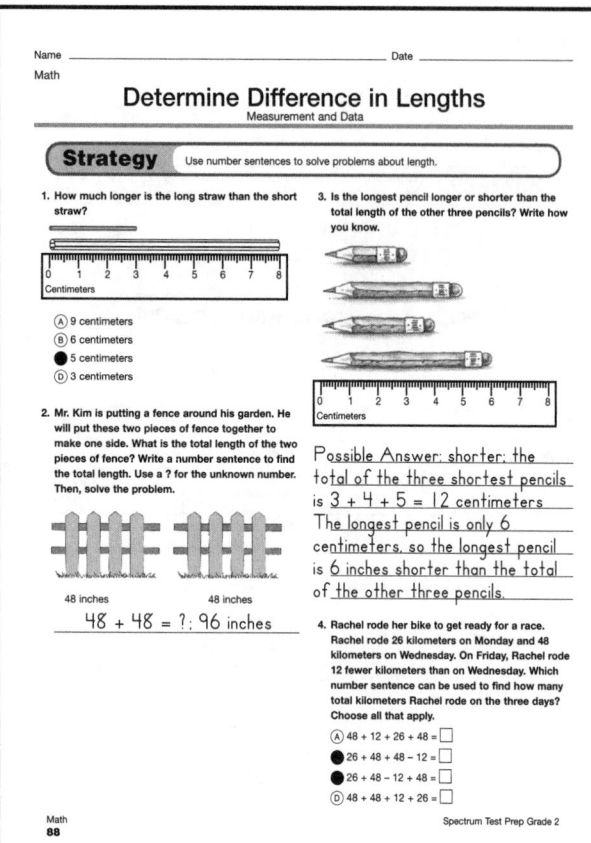

Ⓐ 9 centimeters
Ⓑ 6 centimeters
● 5 centimeters
Ⓓ 3 centimeters

2. Mr. Kim is putting a fence around his garden. He will put these two pieces of fence together to make one side. What is the total length of the two pieces of fence? Write a number sentence to find the total length. Use a ? for the unknown number. Then, solve the problem.

48 inches   48 inches

48 + 48 = ?; 96 inches

3. Is the longest pencil longer or shorter than the total length of the other three pencils? Write how you know.

Possible Answer: shorter; the total of the three shortest pencils is 3 + 4 + 5 = 12 centimeters. The longest pencil is only 6 centimeters, so the longest pencil is 6 inches shorter than the total of the other three pencils.

4. Rachel rode her bike to get ready for a race. Rachel rode 26 kilometers on Monday and 48 kilometers on Wednesday. On Friday, Rachel rode 12 fewer kilometers than on Wednesday. Which number sentence can be used to find how many total kilometers Rachel rode on the three days? Choose all that apply.

Ⓐ 48 + 12 + 26 + 48 = ▢
● 26 + 48 + 48 − 12 = ▢
● 26 + 48 − 12 + 48 = ▢
Ⓓ 48 + 48 + 12 + 26 = ▢

88

Telling Time
Measurement and Data

Strategy Use analog and digital clocks to solve problems about time.

Test Tip Remember that some clocks use the short hand to show the hour and the long hand to show the minutes.

EXAMPLE

How are the clocks alike? Choose all that apply.

Clock A   Clock B

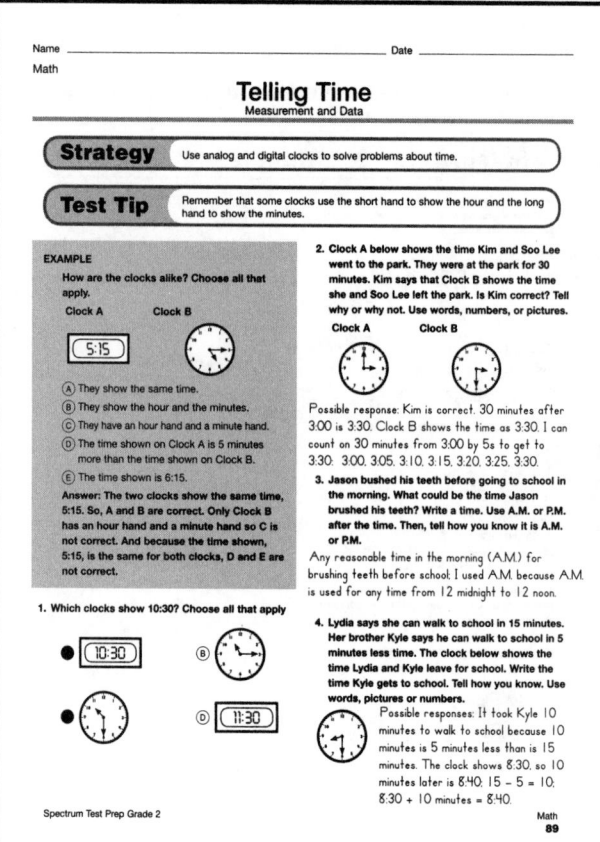

Ⓐ They show the same time.
Ⓑ They show the hour and the minutes.
Ⓒ They have an hour hand and a minute hand.
Ⓓ The time shown on Clock A is 5 minutes more than the time shown on Clock B.
Ⓔ The time shown is 6:15.

Answer: The two clocks show the same time, 5:15. So, A and B are correct. Only Clock B has an hour hand and a minute hand so C is not correct. And because the time shown, 5:15, is the same for both clocks, D and E are not correct.

1. Which clocks show 10:30? Choose all that apply.

2. Clock A below shows the time Kim and Soo Lee went to the park. They were at the park for 30 minutes. Kim says that Clock B shows the time she and Soo Lee left the park. Is Kim correct? Tell why or why not. Use words, numbers, or pictures.

Clock A   Clock B

Possible response: Kim is correct. 30 minutes after 3:00 is 3:30. Clock B shows the time as 3:30. I can count on 30 minutes from 3:00 by 5s to get to 3:30: 3:00, 3:05, 3:10, 3:15, 3:20, 3:25, 3:30.

3. Jason brushed his teeth before going to school in the morning. What could be the time Jason brushed his teeth? Write a time. Use A.M. or P.M. after the time. Then, tell how you know it is A.M. or P.M.

Any reasonable time in the morning (A.M.) for brushing teeth before school; I used A.M. because A.M. is used for any time from 12 midnight to 12 noon.

4. Lydia says she can walk to school in 15 minutes. Her brother Kyle says he can walk to school in 5 minutes less time. The clock below shows the time Lydia and Kyle leave for school. Write the time Kyle gets to school. Tell how you know. Use words, pictures or numbers.

Possible responses: It took Kyle 10 minutes to walk to school because 10 minutes is 5 minutes less than is 15 minutes. The clock shows 8:30, so 10 minutes later is 8:40. 15 − 5 = 10; 8:30 + 10 minutes = 8:40.

89

Solve Problems: Money
Measurement and Data

DIRECTIONS: Answer the questions.

Strategy Use counting, adding, and subtracting to solve money word problems involving dollar bills, quarters, dimes, nickels, and pennies.

EXAMPLE

Notebooks at the school store cost 60¢ each. Pens cost 35¢ each. Hal has the coins below. Does he have enough money to buy one pen and one notebook? Write how you know.

Answer: No. Hal needs 95¢ and the coins show on 85¢.

1. Michael has 4 quarters and 2 dimes for bus fare. If the bus ride costs 75¢, how much money will he have left?

Ⓐ 75¢
● 45¢
Ⓒ 20¢
Ⓓ 70¢

2. Arnie wants to buy 3 books. Each book costs $1.00. Arnie has the money shown below. Does he have enough money to buy the books? Write how you know. How much will it cost to pay for all the books?

Arnie has enough money. He has $4 and the 3 books cost $1 each for a total of $3.

3. Rayna wants to buy a toy that costs one dollar. She has the coins below. How much more money does she need? Choose all that apply.

4. Melinda has the money shown below. Draw coins to show the same amount 2 more ways.

Any combination of coins that total 43 cents; for example, 4 dimes and 3 pennies; 6 nickels, 1 dime, 3 pennies.

90

Represent and Interpret Data: Line Plots
Measurement and Data

DIRECTIONS: Choose or write the correct answer.

Strategy Use line plots by representing measurements to answer questions.

1. Luann measured some lengths of ribbon. The line plot shows the measurements. What is true about the measurements?

Luann's Ribbons

Ⓐ There are more ribbons longer than 3 inches than shorter than 3 inches.
Ⓑ The longest ribbons are 2 inches long.
Ⓒ There are no ribbons longer than 1 inch.
● There is 1 ribbon that is 4 inches long.

2. Kevin measured the lengths of the paper chains he made. He recorded the results in a line plot. How many of the paper chains are 4 feet long?

Kevin's Paper Chains

2 chains

DIRECTIONS: Jonas measures some boards he will use to build a dog house. The lengths are shown in the line plot below. Use the line plot to answer questions 3–5.

Board Lengths

3. How many boards does Jonas have?

● 15
Ⓑ 8
Ⓒ 50
Ⓓ 20

4. Jonas says that the line plot shows that there is only one board more than 11 feet long. Write two more statements that are true about the line plot.

Possible Answer: There are more boards less than 10 feet long than greater than 10 feet long. Two boards are 9 feet long.

5. Jonas needs 5 boards that are greater than 10 feet long. Does he have what he needs? Write how you know.

Possible Answer: Jonas has what he needs. The line plot shows there are 5 boards greater than 10 feet long.

91

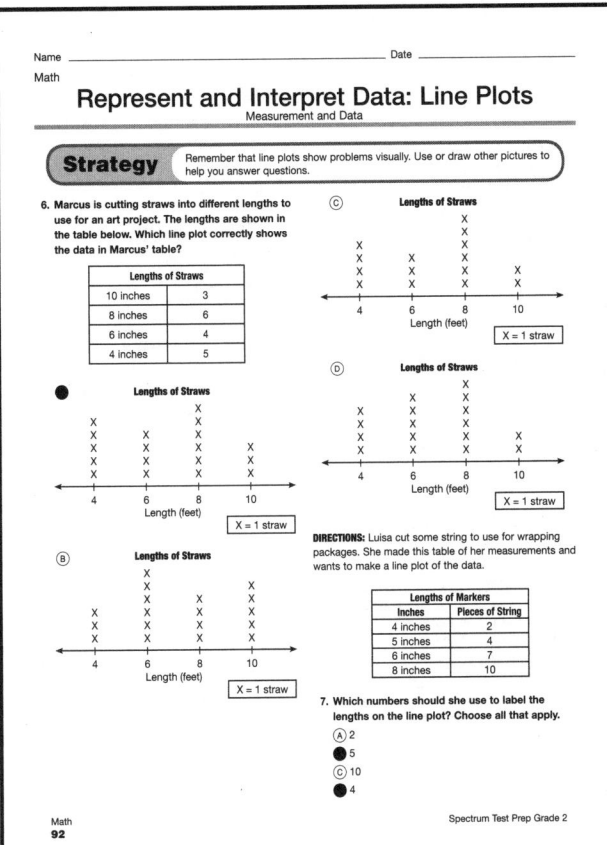

92

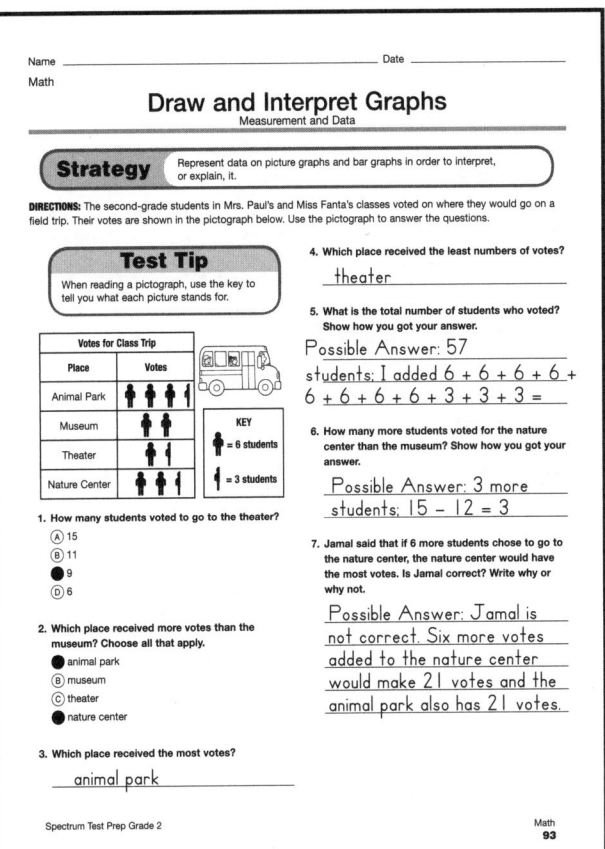

93

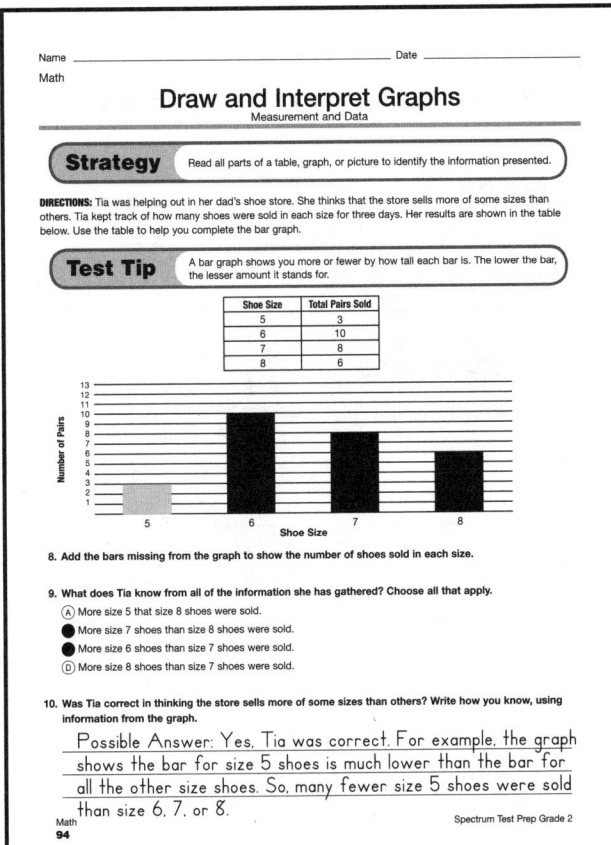

94

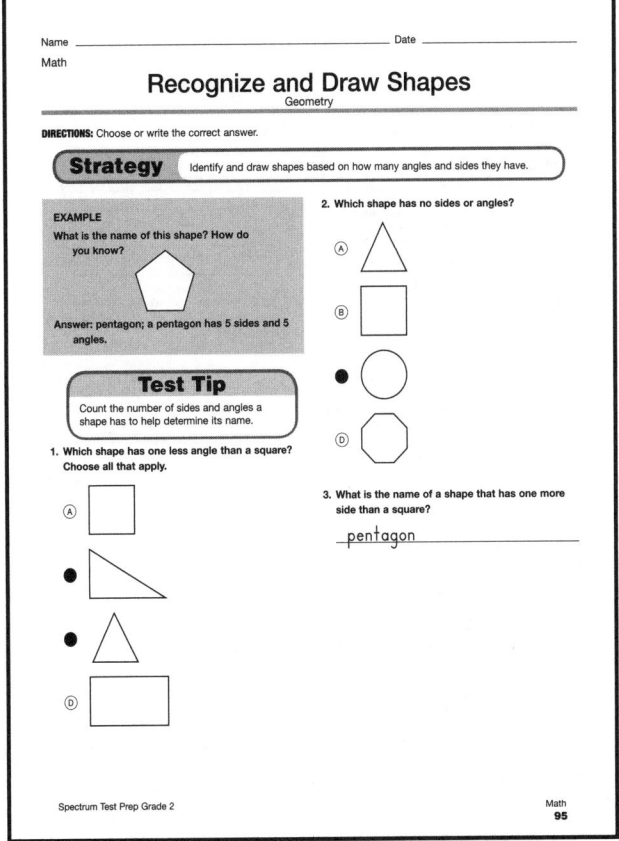

95

Name _____ Date _____
Math

Recognize and Draw Shapes
Geometry

Strategy Make a table of each shape, drawing the shape, writing its name, and then writing the number of sides.

DIRECTIONS: Use the shapes inside the box to answer questions 4 and 5.

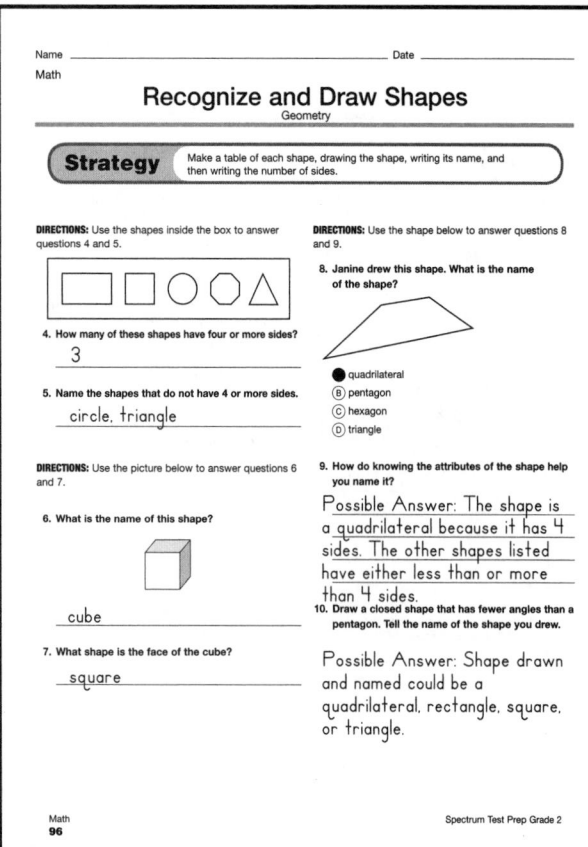

4. How many of these shapes have four or more sides?

3

5. Name the shapes that do not have 4 or more sides.

circle, triangle

DIRECTIONS: Use the picture below to answer questions 6 and 7.

6. What is the name of this shape?

cube

7. What shape is the face of the cube?

square

DIRECTIONS: Use the shape below to answer questions 8 and 9.

8. Janine drew this shape. What is the name of the shape?

● quadrilateral
Ⓑ pentagon
Ⓒ hexagon
Ⓓ triangle

9. How do knowing the attributes of the shape help you name it?

Possible Answer: The shape is a quadrilateral because it has 4 sides. The other shapes listed have either less than or more than 4 sides.

10. Draw a closed shape that has fewer angles than a pentagon. Tell the name of the shape you drew.

Possible Answer: Shape drawn and named could be a quadrilateral, rectangle, square, or triangle.

96

Name _____ Date _____
Math

Partition Rectangles
Geometry

DIRECTIONS: Choose or write the correct answer.

Strategy Use shapes and equal parts to divide rectangles into same-size squares and determine the total number of squares.

EXAMPLE

Daro divided the shape below into equal parts. How many equal parts are in the shape?

Answer: 8 equal parts

Test Tip

Pay attention to the numbers in the problem and the answer choices. If you misread even one number, you may choose the wrong answer.

3. Liam counted 12 small squares in a rectangle. Make a drawing of the rectangle Liam might have seen. Use a ruler to draw your lines.

Possible Answer: drawing of a rectangle partitioned into 12 equal-size squares

1. Ava divided a rectangle into 6 equal parts. Which of these shows Ava's rectangle?

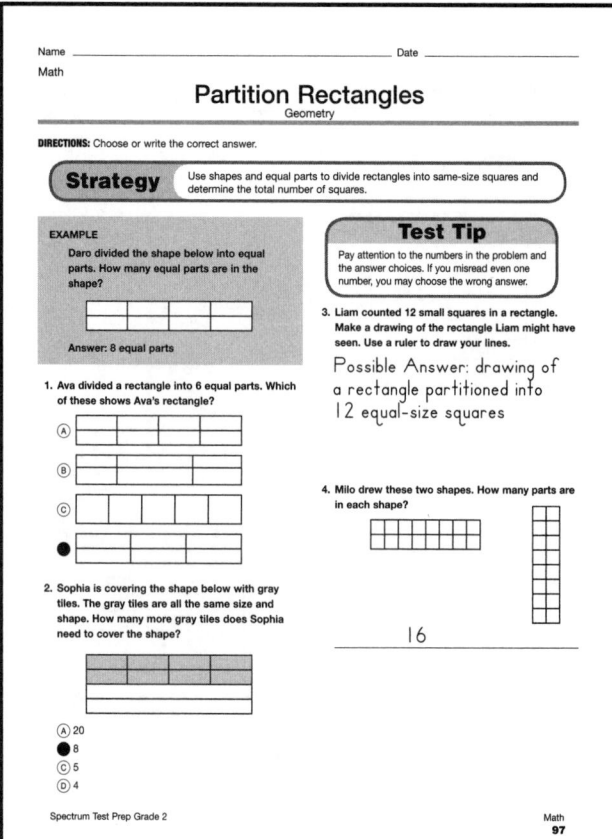

Ⓐ

Ⓑ

Ⓒ

●

4. Milo drew these two shapes. How many parts are in each shape?

16

2. Sophia is covering the shape below with gray tiles. The gray tiles are all the same size and shape. How many more gray tiles does Sophia need to cover the shape?

Ⓐ 20
● 8
Ⓒ 5
Ⓓ 4

97

Name _____ Date _____
Math

Partition Rectangles
Geometry

Strategy Compare shapes to find similarities, such as the number of sides. Use your comparisons to understand how shapes fit within other shapes.

5. Draw lines on the rectangle below to show the same number of equal parts. Use a ruler to draw your lines.

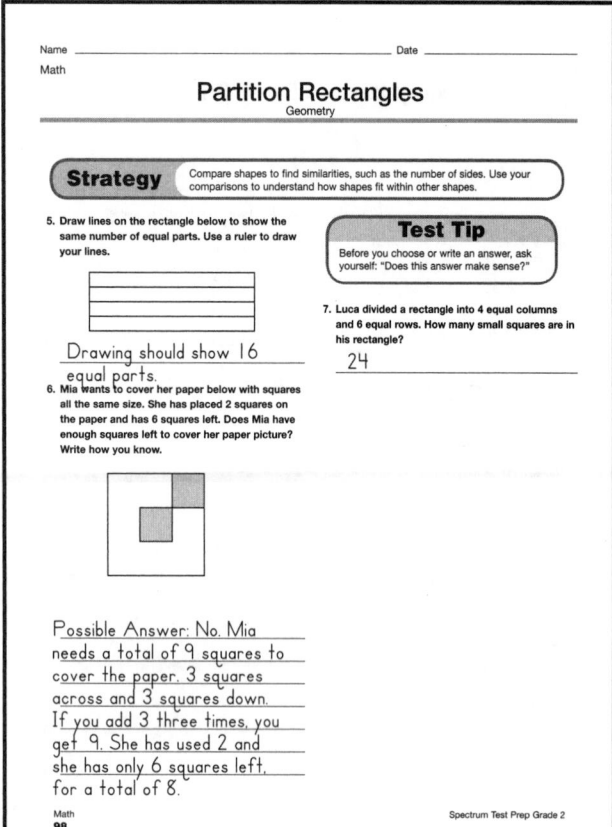

Drawing should show 16 equal parts.

6. Mia wants to cover her paper below with squares all the same size. She has placed 2 squares on the paper and has 6 squares left. Does Mia have enough squares left to cover her paper picture? Write how you know.

Test Tip

Before you choose or write an answer, ask yourself: "Does this answer make sense?"

7. Luca divided a rectangle into 4 equal columns and 6 equal rows. How many small squares are in his rectangle?

24

Possible Answer: No. Mia needs a total of 9 squares to cover the paper. 3 squares across and 3 squares down. If you add 3 three times, you get 9. She has used 2 and she has only 6 squares left, for a total of 8.

98

Name _____ Date _____
Math

Partition Circles and Rectangles Equally
Geometry

DIRECTIONS: Choose or write the correct answer.

Strategy Use the attributes of circles and rectangles to divide them into equal shares and describe the shares using halves, thirds, and fourths.

EXAMPLE

How many equal shares are in this rectangle?
What are the shares called?
How many shares make up the whole?

Answer: 4 equal shares. The shares are called fourths. The whole is four fourths.

1. How many parts does this circle have?

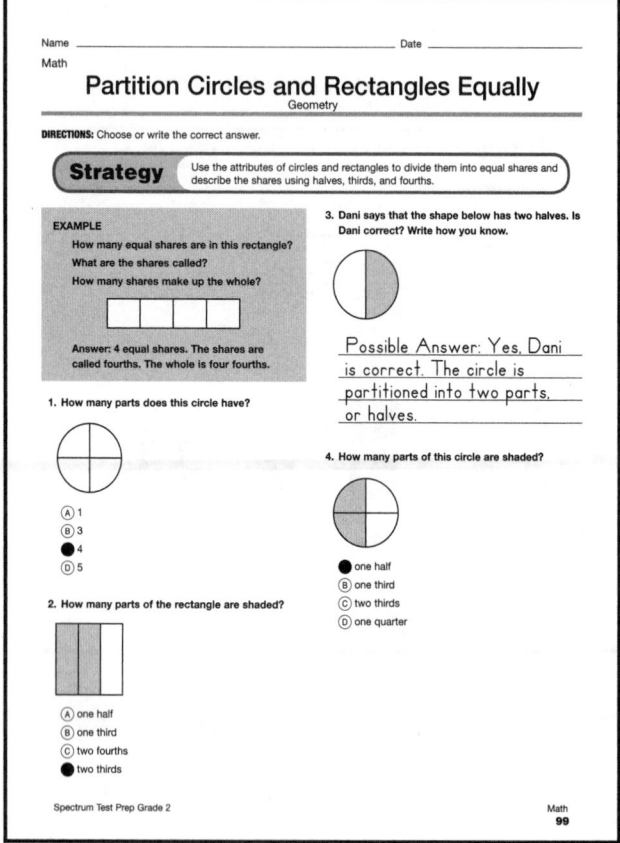

Ⓐ 1
Ⓑ 3
● 4
Ⓓ 5

2. How many parts of the rectangle are shaded?

Ⓐ one half
Ⓑ one third
Ⓒ two fourths
● two thirds

3. Dani says that the shape below has two halves. Is Dani correct? Write how you know.

Possible Answer: Yes, Dani is correct. The circle is partitioned into two parts, or halves.

4. How many parts of this circle are shaded?

● one half
Ⓑ one third
Ⓒ two thirds
Ⓓ one quarter

99

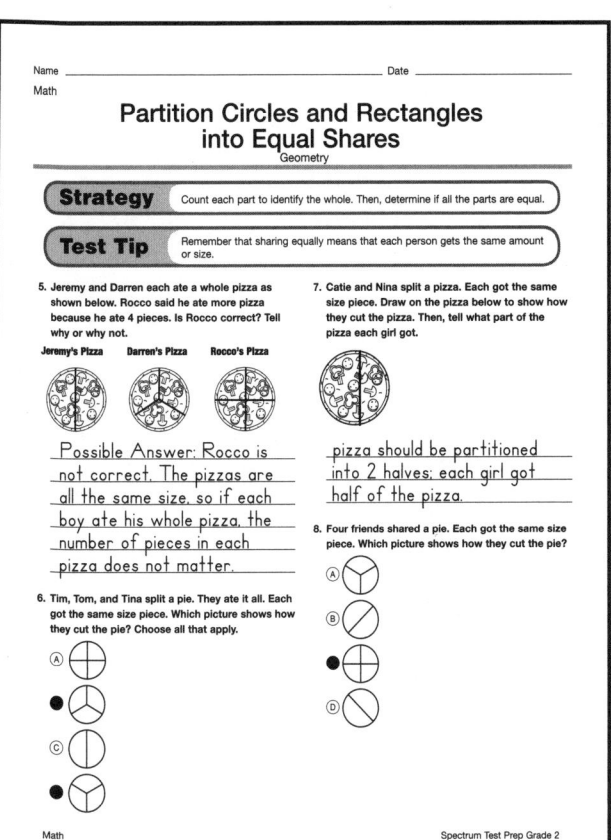

Page 100:

Partition Circles and Rectangles into Equal Shares
Geometry

Strategy — Count each part to identify the whole. Then, determine if all the parts are equal.

Test Tip — Remember that sharing equally means that each person gets the same amount or size.

5. Jeremy and Darren each ate a whole pizza as shown below. Rocco said he ate more pizza because he ate 4 pieces. Is Rocco correct? Tell why or why not.

Jeremy's Pizza   Darren's Pizza   Rocco's Pizza

Possible Answer: Rocco is not correct. The pizzas are all the same size, so if each boy ate his whole pizza, the number of pieces in each pizza does not matter.

6. Tim, Tom, and Tina split a pie. They ate it all. Each got the same size piece. Which picture shows how they cut the pie? Choose all that apply.

Ⓐ
●
Ⓒ
●

7. Catie and Nina split a pizza. Each got the same size piece. Draw on the pizza below to show how they cut the pizza. Then, tell what part of the pizza each girl got.

pizza should be partitioned into 2 halves; each girl got half of the pizza.

8. Four friends shared a pie. Each got the same size piece. Which picture shows how they cut the pie?

Ⓐ
Ⓑ
●
Ⓓ

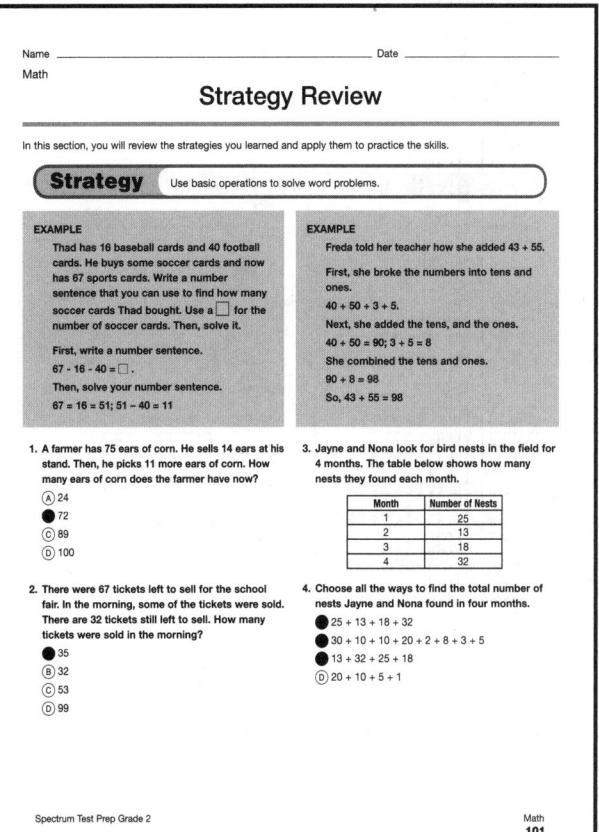

Page 101:

Strategy Review

In this section, you will review the strategies you learned and apply them to practice the skills.

Strategy — Use basic operations to solve word problems.

EXAMPLE
Thad has 16 baseball cards and 40 football cards. He buys some soccer cards and now has 67 sports cards. Write a number sentence that you can use to find how many soccer cards Thad bought. Use a ☐ for the number of soccer cards. Then, solve it.

First, write a number sentence.
67 - 16 - 40 = ☐.
Then, solve your number sentence.
67 - 16 = 51; 51 - 40 = 11

EXAMPLE
Freda told her teacher how she added 43 + 55.

First, she broke the numbers into tens and ones.
40 + 50 + 3 + 5.
Next, she added the tens, and the ones.
40 + 50 = 90; 3 + 5 = 8
She combined the tens and ones.
90 + 8 = 98
So, 43 + 55 = 98

1. A farmer has 75 ears of corn. He sells 14 ears at his stand. Then, he picks 11 more ears of corn. How many ears of corn does the farmer have now?
Ⓐ 24
● 72
Ⓒ 89
Ⓓ 100

2. There were 67 tickets left to sell for the school fair. In the morning, some of the tickets were sold. There are 32 tickets still left to sell. How many tickets were sold in the morning?
● 35
Ⓑ 32
Ⓒ 53
Ⓓ 99

3. Jayne and Nona look for bird nests in the field for 4 months. The table below shows how many nests they found each month.

Month	Number of Nests
1	25
2	13
3	18
4	32

4. Choose all the ways to find the total number of nests Jayne and Nona found in four months.
● 25 + 13 + 18 + 32
● 30 + 10 + 10 + 20 + 2 + 8 + 3 + 5
● 13 + 32 + 25 + 18
Ⓓ 20 + 10 + 5 + 1

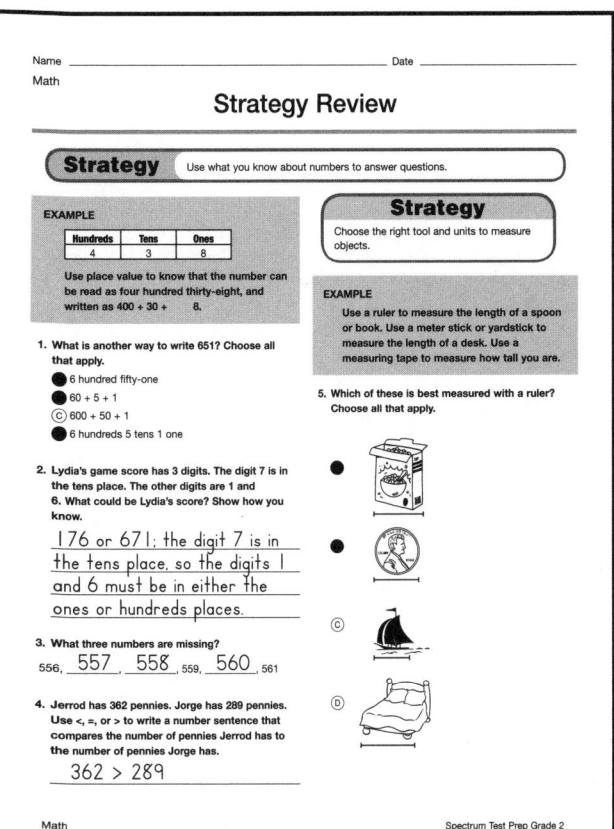

Page 102:

Strategy Review

Strategy — Use what you know about numbers to answer questions.

EXAMPLE

Hundreds	Tens	Ones
4	3	8

Use place value to know that the number can be read as four hundred thirty-eight, and written as 400 + 30 + 8.

1. What is another way to write 651? Choose all that apply.
● 6 hundred fifty-one
● 60 + 5 + 1
Ⓒ 600 + 50 + 1
● 6 hundreds 5 tens 1 one

2. Lydia's game score has 3 digits. The digit 7 is in the tens place. The other digits are 1 and 6. What could be Lydia's score? Show how you know.

176 or 671; the digit 7 is in the tens place, so the digits 1 and 6 must be in either the ones or hundreds places.

3. What three numbers are missing?
556, 557, 558, 559, 560, 561

4. Jerrod has 362 pennies. Jorge has 289 pennies. Use <, =, or > to write a number sentence that compares the number of pennies Jerrod has to the number of pennies Jorge has.

362 > 289

Strategy — Choose the right tool and units to measure objects.

EXAMPLE
Use a ruler to measure the length of a spoon or book. Use a meter stick or yardstick to measure the length of a desk. Use a measuring tape to measure how tall you are.

5. Which of these is best measured with a ruler? Choose all that apply.

●
●
Ⓒ
Ⓓ

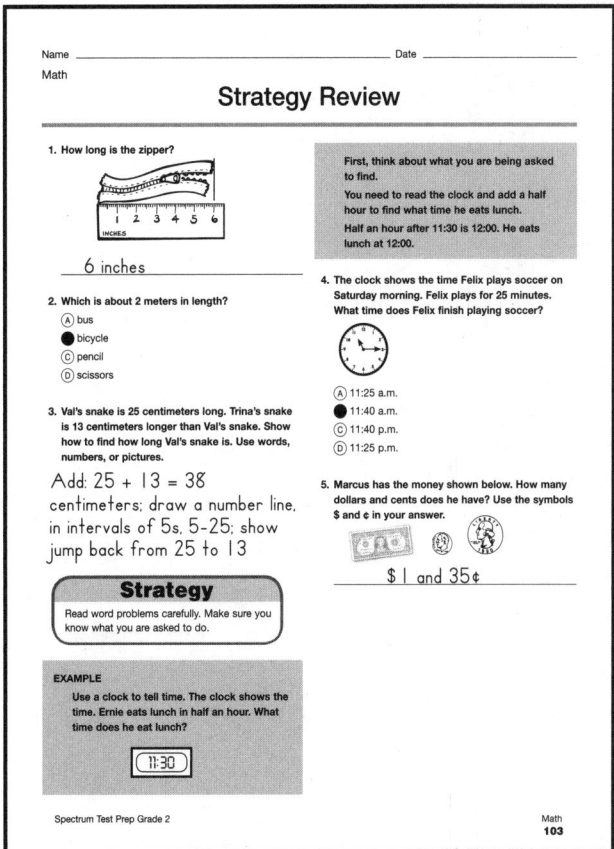

Page 103:

Strategy Review

1. How long is the zipper?

6 inches

2. Which is about 2 meters in length?
Ⓐ bus
● bicycle
Ⓒ pencil
Ⓓ scissors

3. Val's snake is 25 centimeters long. Trina's snake is 13 centimeters longer than Val's snake. Show how to find how long Val's snake is. Use words, numbers, or pictures.

Add: 25 + 13 = 38 centimeters; draw a number line, in intervals of 5s, 5-25; show jump back from 25 to 13

Strategy — Read word problems carefully. Make sure you know what you are asked to do.

EXAMPLE
Use a clock to tell time. The clock shows the time. Ernie eats lunch in half an hour. What time does he eat lunch?

11:30

First, think about what you are being asked to find.
You need to read the clock and add a half hour to find what time he eats lunch.
Half an hour after 11:30 is 12:00. He eats lunch at 12:00.

4. The clock shows the time Felix plays soccer on Saturday morning. Felix plays for 25 minutes. What time does Felix finish playing soccer?

Ⓐ 11:25 a.m.
● 11:40 a.m.
Ⓒ 11:40 p.m.
Ⓓ 11:25 p.m.

5. Marcus has the money shown below. How many dollars and cents does he have? Use the symbols $ and ¢ in your answer.

$ 1 and 35¢

Name ______________________ Date ______________
Math

Strategy Review

DIRECTIONS: Use the picture graph below to answer the questions.

Strategy

Use graphs and drawings to understand numbers.

EXAMPLE

A picture graph uses symbols or pictures in place of a number. The key tells what number each picture stands for. How many students does each 🯅 stand for in the key below?

ey: 🯅 students Answer: 5 students

Grade Level	Number of Students
Kindergarten	🯅🯅🯅🯅🯅🯅🯅🯅🯅
1st Grade	🯅🯅🯅🯅🯅🯅🯅🯅🯅🯅🯅🯅
2nd Grade	🯅🯅🯅🯅🯅🯅
3rd Grade	🯅🯅🯅🯅🯅🯅🯅🯅
4th Grade	🯅🯅🯅🯅🯅🯅🯅🯅🯅🯅🯅🯅
5th Grade	🯅🯅🯅🯅🯅🯅🯅

Key: 🯅 = 5 students

1. **What grade level has the fewest students? Write how you know.**

2nd grade; it has the fewest number of symbols in the graph

2. **How many more students are in 1st grade than in 3rd grade? Show your work.**

20 more; count by 5s to find 60 students in first grade and 40 in third grade. So, 60 – 40 = 20.

Strategy

Use what ou know about numbers shapes and measurement to answer questions.

EXAMPLE

Name the shape that has these attributes:
- **4 equal sides**
- **4 equal angles**

The shape is a square.

DIRECTIONS: Gia and Malani each cut out some shapes to make a picture. One of the shapes is shown below. Use the shapes to answer questions 1 and 2.

Gia's

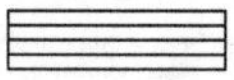

Malani's

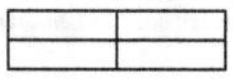

3. **What is the name of the shape the girls cut out? Write how you know.**

rectangle; it has 4 sides and 4 same-size angles

4. **Malani thinks her pieces are larger than Gia's. Is she correct? Why or why not?**

The pieces are the same size because the shapes are the same size, and cutting each into four equal pieces makes each piece an equal share.

Math
104

Spectrum Test Prep Grade 2

104